Cooking in harmony with nature

AT HOME WITH AYURVEDA

The Science of Living Cookery Book

Linda

Sandra x

Linda Bretherton & Sandra Czachur

At Home with Ayurveda
The Science of Living Cookery Book
By Linda Bretherton & Sandra Czachur

First published in 2024
ISBN 978-1-0686594-0-9

Design and typesetting by Fountain Creative Ltd.

TAUK
Publishing

CONTENTS

WHO ARE WE?

I have been involved in Ayurveda for over 35 years, as a consultant, practitioner, spent 10 years as a Master Trainer teaching practitioners, owned an Ayurvedic Spa and Clinic and ran an Ayurvedic restaurant and cooked for thousands on retreats and workshops. This book represents many of the much-loved recipes.

In my younger days I was an interior designer and now work with Vastu Shastra which means 'The Science of Dwelling' which is how I like to keep my kitchen based on these principles. I am a mother, wife and an avid animal lover. I am also known as Vani – a name bestowed upon me by my Vedic mentor during my training in a monastery.

This book has been a long time coming and one that was dependant on great photography, which is where Sandra with her many talents came in to join me in preparing the pages. Sandra came on one of the practitioner programmes that I ran many years ago, we became friends through our many mutual activities and in this instance our love of food brought us on this journey, Sandra is the second taster, after me, for all the recipes in this book. She is also a major influencer on Instagram @homesweetholmedale, a mother, Granny, wife, and a dog & cat Mummy.

Although Ayurveda means The Science of Life (Ayur means life, Veda means science or knowledge) to me it represents the 'science of living'.

It offers us all a remarkable body of wisdom designed to help us stay vibrant and healthy while realising our full human potential. Providing us with guidelines on ideal daily and seasonal routines, diet, behaviour, and the proper use of our senses,

Ayurveda reminds us that health is the balanced and dynamic integration between our environment, body, mind, and spirit.

Ayurveda is considered to be a 7,000 year old system of natural healing originating from the Vedic culture of India, it is just as potent today in our fast paced lives. You are invited to bring the wonderful ways of Ayurveda food into your daily lives, Ayurveda reminds us that your kitchen is your pharmacy!

There are hundreds of books about Ayurveda and although we have provided you with some background information, it really is just a glimpse into this fascinating world. My book *Dosha for Life* is a comprehensive introduction to how Ayurveda works in your body and mind.

Ayurveda reminds us throughout its many modalities that we are at one with nature and the universal energies that surround us within and without. We are affected by everything including the time of day and the changing seasons and in simple terms we are encouraged to buy and eat our food from local producers and eat food that is in alignment with the time of year. Our appetites and digestive functions differ according to which season we are in, briefly Vata season is autumn, Pitta season is summer and Kapha season is Spring.

All the recipes have been chosen from the many that I cook on my retreats and workshops and ones that are loved and enjoyed by many.

Ayurveda recommends that we eat meat free, organic and local foods for optimum health. But what if we find ourselves in situations that do not allow us to have access to these options? I have included a variety of recipes which use dried products that you can use during these times. Keep your dried produce in airtight containers to keep them fresh for as long as possible. Keep spices in their seed format so that you can grind them as and when needed. I've also included tinned products for the same reason.

I hope that you enjoy these recipes and both Sandra and I wish you only the very best in your Ayurveda journey of food and cookery.

Namaste

Linda/Vani & Sandra

BAILEY ST.
LONDON

THE MAGIC OF AYURVEDA

WHAT IS AYURVEDA?

Directly translated, Ayurveda means 'The Science of Life'. It is one of the oldest forms of healing the world has known, with its origins dating back over 7,000 years. Ayurveda is one of the most profound health practices in the world. Ayurveda is a system of preventative healthcare and healing and a philosophy for living. It cures not by simply treating the symptoms but by removing the causes of disease and, critically, by balancing the physical and spiritual elements of our lives. The objective is to achieve balance as an individual, as one whose emotional life, intake of food, output of energy and attention to the daily act of living is also extended to take in the wider concept of a harmonious universe.

As fundamental today as it was 7,000 years ago, it is the central concept of balance and harmony between all living things. Within Ayurveda, the Earth is seen to be an interrelated whole, a vast living organism. We share the same atomic and molecular structures and the same building blocks as all life forms, what happens to one part affects the whole. Our world is a wonderful living entity: the atmosphere that we live in, the oxygen, the weather systems, the natural resources, the earth and the sea, and the animal and plant life are all connected.

THE FIVE ELEMENTS

Ayurveda sees the world composed of five elements: ether/space, air, fire, water and earth. Each and every living thing is composed of these elements.

These five elements are within all living things in the form of vital energies that can fluctuate according to our state of balance and the seasons of nature, thus affecting health.

We have the elements of Space, Air, Fire, Water and Earth within our bodies in the form of acids, enzymes, fluids, tissues, the movement and function of muscles and organs. These elements and our pulse of life are sustained by nutrition in the very broadest sense, which we obtain from food, breathing and the attention we give to ourselves.

The key factors that influence our quality of life, for good or bad, are food, exercise and activity, our home and working environments, and the way we use our mind and senses. Dramatic changes to our outlook, health and energy happen as a result of what we put into our hearts, minds and bodies.

Our bodies rebuild themselves many times throughout our lifetime. Cells from every organ are renewed by the food that we eat, every breath that we take, every mouthful that we swallow, they all contribute to this building process. Every taste, sight and smell, in fact, every sensory experience connected with food, rebuilds or damages our cells and imprints itself into our emotions and the sensory experience of being alive.

BODY TYPES OR DOSHAS

People come in so many shapes, sizes, colours and weights. It seems obvious that we shouldn't all eat and do the same things to make us healthy and happy. We are all individuals with different tastes and experiences.

Physical differences can be important clues, but they don't tell us about emotional characteristics or behaviour. Why do some people never gain weight while others can never shake it off? Why are some constant worriers while others struggle to rouse themselves into action? We suffer from all kinds of ailments, yet despite this wide range of people types, the differences in how we react to food, our surroundings and each other are treated by the mainstream health industry in broad brushstrokes.

So yes, there are great differences between people, but fortunately, there is also a map to guide us, this is the questionnaire that guides us through the maze of types and helps us to make sense of our ayurvedic constitution. There are common factors formed from the five elements of ether/space, air, fire, water and earth. These elements form unique balances within each individual to create their body type or dosha. No two people are the same; we all have the same ingredients but in differing quantities.

With Ayurveda, we learn how to recognise the balance of elements that make our dosha and how to respond to their dynamics.

In Ayurveda, our body type, or dosha, provides the key to understanding who we are, allowing us to examine and fine-tune our diets and lifestyles to create health, strength and energy for life. Our doshas have clearly defined characteristics and specific nutritional, emotional and spiritual needs. Our preferences for food, colour, tastes, textures, sounds and activities are founded upon this cellular make-up.

Certain kinds of foods are more useful to us than others. We are also better suited to certain sounds, textures, colours, smells, oils and environments. We react physically and emotionally to the changing seasons and climate in different ways according to our dosha. How we function and behave, how we respond to these elements in our daily lives, and how our emotions fluctuate are all affected by this metabolic template within us. When we live, eat, and do things that go against the best interest of our body type, we are actively damaging everything that we are!

AYURVEDA DEFINES THREE MAIN DOSHAS CREATED BY THE ENERGY FORCES OF ETHER/SPACE, AIR, FIRE, WATER, AND EARTH WITHIN US.

VATA, the most common dosha, consists of air and ether/space and works with the nervous system to control all body movement, including nutrients and waste. In the mind, Vata is connected to our memory and comparison of information. Air is the breath which stimulates movement. Ether/space is the stillness where the vibration of all vital systems and creative activity occurs.

PITTA consists of fire and water. It governs the body's balance of chemical and transforming energies, including the digestion of both food and thought. In the mind, Pitta processes new data and draws conclusions. Fire is the acids and enzymes of the body and the sun's rays that directly affect all life forms and the environment. Water is the fluid present in every cell, and it can be calm or turbulent.

KAPHA consists of earth and water and governs structure, bodily stability, lubrication and cell structure. In the mind, Kapha provides stability and the ability to grasp single thoughts. The earth is our physical body and is solid and grounding. Water is the fluid present in every cell, and when mixed with earth, it can become dense and heavy.

The nourishing elements in our food are the same elements that we are composed of. Our food, which contains the elements of ether/space, air, fire, water, and earth, has an inheritance that passes on to us in the continual rebuilding process of life.

We don't have to think about it because it's an automatic process that we take for granted. All it needs is the best building blocks for our particular combination of elements.

DOSHA QUESTIONNAIRE

This questionnaire will help you to determine your own Prakruti/body type according to Ayurveda. It is meant to be general, and the characteristics are based upon your 'natural' state and lifelong physical and emotional states. Be completely honest with your answers, and ask someone to help you if you are not sure. For each column, go across horizontally and circle each characteristic that is applicable to you. Go through all the columns: Vata, Pitta and Kapha.

At the bottom of the columns, add up your scores. The totals will help determine your particular body type. For example, if you have 25 Vata, 15 Pitta and 8 Kapha, your body type will be Vata/Pitta. Everyone has all three doshas in their constitution, and the highest number will be your most current prominent one, with a closer second. Very few people are tridosha, where all doshas are equal.

1. UPPER BODY

YOURSELF	VATA		PITTA		KAPHA	
BODY FRAME	Thin, irregular, very short or very tall, bony, slender or rangy.	☐	Medium, proportionate, toned, average frame.	☐	Heavy, broad, stocky, stout, well-developed.	☐
BONES / FRAME	Thin, small.	☐	Average.	☐	Large.	☐
JOINTS	Small, cracking, prominent, dry, thin.	☐	Medium, loose.	☐	Large, well-built.	☐
WEIGHT	Hard to gain weight, easy to lose, low, protruding veins and bones, fluctuating weight.	☐	Easy to gain, easy to lose, moderate, muscular.	☐	Easy to gain, hard to lose, heavy, tends to be obese.	☐
UPPER BODY	Small, narrow, hard to gain weight, unproportioned.	☐	Medium, well-proportioned.	☐	Large, well-developed, broad, gains weight easily.	☐
SHOULDERS	Thin, flat, hunched.	☐	Medium.	☐	Strong, broad, thick.	☐
ARMS	Bony elbows, long, thin, small.	☐	Average, wiry.	☐	Big, heavy, well-developed, fleshy.	☐
HANDS	Small, long, narrow, bony knuckles, cool, rough, dry.	☐	Medium, warm, hot, sticky.	☐	Large, solid, cool, square.	☐
FINGERS	Long, tapered.	☐	Medium.	☐	Short and squarish.	☐
NAILS	Small, thin, dry, rough, cracking, dark.	☐	Soft pink, pliable, medium shape.	☐	Wide, large, thick, white, smooth, firm.	☐

2. LOWER BODY

YOURSELF	VATA		PITTA		KAPHA	
THIGHS	Thin, narrow, bony.	☐	Medium proportion to body.	☐	Cellulite, well-developed, fat.	☐
LEGS	Thin, bony knees, very short or very long, co-ordination can be unsteady.	☐	Averagely proportioned legs.	☐	Stable, thick, stocky with standing power.	☐
CALVES	Slim, tight, wiry.	☐	Medium proportion, soft, loose.	☐	Large, shapely, firm.	☐
FEET	Long or very small, thin, rough, dry, unsteady, long toes, cool.	☐	Average size, soft pink, normal to warm, hot, sweaty.	☐	Large, thick, steady, normally warm.	☐

3. FACE AND HEAD

YOURSELF	VATA		PITTA		KAPHA	
HEAD	Long or small, thin, can be unsteady or have stiff neck.	☐	Average, proportioned, steady.	☐	Big, square, stocky, steady.	☐
HAIR	Curly/frizzy, dry, coarse, split hair.	☐	Red, blonde, straight, early grey, bald, soft and fine.	☐	Thick, wavy, dark, oily, shiny.	☐
FOREHEAD	Small forehead with wrinkles.	☐	Average forehead with horizontal folds.	☐	Broad forehead and thick.	☐
FACE	Small or long, thin and sallow, dull and wrinkles easily.	☐	Average shape, sharp contours, pinkish.	☐	Big, round, flattish, pale, soft features.	☐
SKIN	Dry, cool, thin, rough, cracked, prominent veins. More difficult to sunburn.	☐	Warm, sometimes delicate and sensitive, pink, freckles, acne, moles, spots, rashes, easily sunburns.	☐	Cool, smooth, white, soft, moist, oily, fatty, good in the sun.	☐
COMPLEXION	Dull, darkish without lustre.	☐	Flushed, freckles, glowing.	☐	Pale.	☐
EYES/LASHES/ BROWS	**Eyes**: small, erratic, unsteady and prone to dryness. **Lashes**: short and scanty. **Brows**: large, profuse or very small.	☐	**Eyes**: medium, reddish, green, grey, piercing, light sensitive. **Lashes**:moderate. **Brows**: moderate.	☐	**Eyes**: wide, oily, attractive, can cry easily, steady focus. **Lashes**: lush, long. Brows: strong.	☐
NOSE	Thin, long or very small, pointed, dry, crooked.	☐	Average, pointed, sharp shape.	☐	Big, firm, oily.	☐
LIPS	Narrow, small/large, dry, unsteady, dark.	☐	Medium, soft, red.	☐	Large, thick, oily, smooth, firm.	☐
TEETH AND GUMS	Small or large in size, crooked, rough, dry with spaces, protruding teeth. receding gums.	☐	Average proportioned teeth. Gums soft and pink that bleed easily.	☐	Big, white, square teeth. Soft, pink, strong gums.	☐
MOUTH	Often dry with an astringent taste.	☐	Often salivating, with a bitter, pungent taste.	☐	Excess salivation, with sweet, salty taste and mucus in throat.	☐
THROAT	Constricted throat, rough and dry.	☐	Sore, inflamed and burning.	☐	Swollen, tight.	☐
STOMACH	Excess hiccupping, belching, variable appetite, feelings of constriction.	☐	Burning, sour, pungent belches or hiccups, excess appetite, heartburn.	☐	Sweet or mucus belching, slow digestion, feeling nauseous.	☐
APPETITE	Variable, erratic, irregular, eats quickly, likes warm, oily foods.	☐	Strong, sharp, intense, eats fast, enjoys cold foods.	☐	Low but constant, consistent, eats slowly, likes warm, dry foods.	☐
CIRCULATION	Poor, variable, palpitations, aggravated by wind, dry weather and the cold.	☐	Warm to hot, circulation good, aggravated by heat, fire and sun.	☐	Circulation slow and steady, aggravated by damp and cold.	☐
TASTES	Bitter, astringent and pungent.	☐	Sour, pungent and salty.	☐	Sweet, sour and salty.	☐

4. MENTAL TRAITS

YOURSELF	VATA		PITTA		KAPHA	
SENSITIVITIES	Loud noise.	☐	Bright lights, strong sunlight	☐	Strong odours.	☐
VOICE/SPEAKING	Low, weak, whining, monotone, quick, talkative, rambling, imaginative, varied depending on changing moods.	☐	High, sharp, clear, precise, organised, detailed, orators, moderate, argumentative.	☐	Deep, tonal, singers, slow, silent, drawn-out.	☐
DREAM/SLEEP	Flying, erratic, running, fearful, light sleep.	☐	Fighting, in colour, moderately deep, violent, intense.	☐	Romantic, water, few, heavy, deep sleep, long.	☐
MIND/SENSES	Fear, anxiety, apathy, sorrow, delusion, nervousness, insomnia, needing heat. Strongly dislikes cold things, loss of coordination, indecisive, perceptive.	☐	Violent, delirious, dizzy, fainting, needing cold, poor senses, intoxicated, restlessness, hot-headed, impatient, hot-tempered, critical, angry, arrogant, intelligent.	☐	Calm, lethargic, stupor, excessive sleep, slow perception, desires heat, dull, inert, greedy, stubborn, possessive.	☐
MEMORY/ LEARNING	Quick to learn ideas but also forgets quickly, likes to study many things but becomes unfocused, learns by listening.	☐	Learns quickly, forgets slowly, focused, penetrating, discriminating, goal-oriented, learns best by reading and with visuals.	☐	Slow to learn but never forgets, learns by association, steady.	☐
NATURE	Adaptable, quick, indecisive.	☐	Penetrating, critical, intelligent.	☐	Slow, steady, grounded, flat.	☐
MEMORY	Understands ideas quickly, then forgets quickly.	☐	Clear, sharp, quick and lasting.	☐	Slow to learn, but once learns, never forgets.	☐
FAITH	Erratic, rebellious, changeable, spiritually disciplined.	☐	Leader, goals, fanatical, tendency toward material success.	☐	Loyal, constant, conservative, fundamentally material.	☐
EMOTIONS	Anxious, nervous, fearful, changeable.	☐	Angry, irritable, argumentative, fiery.	☐	Contented, calm, sentimental, slow to anger.	☐
HABITS	Travel, culture, humour, eccentric, obsessive.	☐	Politics, sports, dance, competitive, determined.	☐	Water sports, flowers, cosmetics, business, lazy.	☐
MENTAL DISORDERS	Anxiety attacks, hysteria, trembling.	☐	Rage, tantrums, excess temper.	☐	Depression, sorrow, lethargy.	☐
LIFE PACE	Fast, unsteady, erratic, hyperactive.	☐	Moderate, purposeful, goal-oriented.	☐	Slow, steady.	☐
ENDURANCE	Low or fluctuating.	☐	Moderate to high, heat intolerance, pushes until one burns out.	☐	Strong, steady, slow starters, enduring performance.	☐
SEXUAL NATURE	Variable, strong desire but low energy, cold.	☐	Moderate, passionate, domineering, quarrelsome.	☐	Constant, low, devoted, warm.	☐

5. SYMPTOMS OF DISEASE

YOURSELF	VATA	PITTA	KAPHA
INITIAL SIGNS OF DISEASE	Variable symptoms, irregular and rapid onset. ☐	High temperature/fevers, moderate onset. ☐	Slow but constant onset often from congestion. ☐
DISEASE TENDENCIES	Nervous disorders, immune system diseases, arthritic pains, mental disturbances, stress disturbances, bone and joint problems. ☐	Infections, blood disorders, inflammation, yellow and green mucus. ☐	Problems with respiratory disease, clear, white mucus, obesity. ☐
DISEASE RESISTANCE	Poor resistance to disease, weak immune system. ☐	Moderate resistance to disease, infections and bleeding. ☐	Good resistance to disease, strong immune system. ☐
HEALING/ MEDICINAL REQUIREMENTS/ TENDENCIES	Heals quickly, requires low dosage, has nervous reactions. ☐	Moderate, average. ☐	Slow healing, requires higher dosage. ☐
PAIN	Severe, sharp, disruptive, churning, throbbing, tearing, variable. ☐	Moderate, burning, steaming, swelling, bleeding. ☐	Mild, heavy, dull and constant. ☐
FEVER	Variable, moderate heat, irregular, anxious and restless with a thirst. ☐	High heat, burning thirst, irritable, delirious, sweating. ☐	Low heat, constant, heavy and dull. ☐
DISCHARGES	Gases, cracking joints, bones, sighing, moaning and groaning. ☐	Blood, yellow and green pus, aggressive, angry. ☐	Mucus, clear or white pus, salivation, quiet, stubborn ☐
SWEAT/ODOUR – BASED ON DAILY CLEANSING *(N.B. Vegetarians sweat less than meat eaters.)*	Odourless, scanty. ☐	Strong smell, profuse, hot. ☐	Pleasant smell, moderate when exercising, cold. ☐
FAECES	Scanty, dry, hard, painful, or difficult, gas, constipation. ☐	Abundant, loose, yellowish, burning diarrhoea. (Pitta persons with fevers get constipation.) ☐	Moderate, solid, pale, mucus in stool. (Kaphas may get constipation, but stool is not hard.) ☐
URINE	Scanty, colourless, bubbly, difficult. ☐	Profuse, yellow, red, burning ☐	Moderate, whitish, milky. ☐

TOTALS	VATA	PITTA	KAPHA

VATA

Vata consists of the elements of air and ether/space and is predominantly biased towards movement and change. Vata works with the nervous system to control all body movement, including nutrients and waste. In the mind, Vata is concerned with memory and comparison of information. It is the most common dosha found in daily life, more so over the past 100 years with the increasing levels of change and the frenetic pace that have become the norm in many societies.

VATA HAS PARTICULAR QUALITIES, THESE ARE:

Dry: A Vata type's skin will often be prone to dryness and flakiness. They may lick their fingers before touching paper, wool or dry surfaces and may be slower to perspire compared to others. They may often be thirsty. Dry humour and a tendency to irony are also Vata traits.

Light: Vata skin may be light, dull, or even papery, requiring moisturising and care in all weather conditions, particularly in strong sunlight. Their body weight is usually low, they are slim and often with bony limbs. They may have lightweight hair, often thin and can be light sleepers.

Irregular: A Vata type will have an irregular physique. They can be very tall or very short, they may have thin arms and legs and a strong torso or vice versa, a larger than average head or one that is angular, long or with a small or large chin and a nose that is prominent or small. They may have small eyes, narrow or sunken, dark brown or grey in colour, and irregular teeth. They may suffer from delicate appetites, frequent constipation, or irregular bowel movements and flatulence.

Rough: Unevenness of responses, excessive contrasts and a lack of free flow and smoothness in speech and actions all manifest as roughness with Vata types. Their speech may be lacking in modulation. They may 'feel rough' and show visible signs of wear and tear when fatigued. They may develop rough skin and complexions, especially when older. They may have a 'rough idea' of something and be 'rough and ready' or unkempt and untidy regardless of what they wear.

Roughness can be manifested through coarseness or a lack of softness in everything from behaviour to the texture of skin, clothes and habitat.

Mobile: Vata types never stop moving physically or mentally, and this is often manifested as restlessness. This both strengthens and weakens their natural creativity because the ability to move and shift can lead to creative impulses but also prevent things from being completed. They have strong imaginations and are likely to be artistic or in the creative professions. They often express themselves through sport and are sexually active. Mobility is also manifested as anxiety, fearfulness, questioning and theorising and an ability to spend money easily. When balanced, Vata types achieve many things, and when unbalanced, they appear disconnected from themselves.

Cold: Seasonal change affects Vata types more than others. They feel the cold easily and are susceptible to draughts, yet under the right circumstances and with preparation, they cope with winter weather provided that they wear suitable fleecy clothing. (If they turn up the heating to compensate for the cold, they soon dry out and develop dry, roughened skin.) Vata types can also be emotionally cold, finding it difficult to sustain close relationships. They suit the cooler end of the colour spectrum.

Quick: Vata types think, move, speak and act quickly. They spend quickly, often on the wrong things. They make speedy decisions and are likely to reverse them just as quickly. They fall quickly into agitated states and can be moved quickly out of them, provided awareness is developed. Vata types remember things quickly and forget them quickly.

Changeable: Everything about Vata is changeable. We have already mentioned seasonal change, but it has a profound effect on them more than other doshas because it compounds their inherent changeability. They veer from enthusiasm and intensity to despondency and anxiety, from happiness to joy, from physical balance to uncoordinated chaos, and they do all of this quickly. Their states can change with the speed of a cloud passing across the sun. A Vata type's thought patterns can inspire themselves and all around them or drive everyone to distraction.

Being a Vata type can involve considerable confusion and discomfort when unbalanced. They are creative and welcome new experiences but do not like routine. However, they NEED routine to stabilise their mental patterns and moods. Vata types can easily become out of balance mentally, emotionally and physically and can be indecisive and often fearful in their life environment.

All these qualities increase with age in Vata types.

In our bodies, Vata is responsible for thinking, respiration, circulation and digestive movement. All of these qualities are necessary for all body types, and we wouldn't function without the Vata qualities of movement, nor would we function without the space through which fluids, food and air can pass. These qualities are simply more evident in a Vata type, and they become excessive when Vata become imbalanced.

Vata types are better suited to structured exercise classes such as aerobics or circuit training, swimming, walking, organised jogging, mountain activity, Yoga, Tai Chi and some martial arts activities. They are much less suited to heavy weight-based exercise regimes.

Balanced Vata types are energetic and inspirational, adapt to situations, and are lively, creative and good communicators.

Unbalanced Vata types worry, are agitated, restless and full of anxiety. They are inconsistent and often suffer from insomnia. They can be gassy, bloated and constipated.

A typical Vata stress response is, "What did I do wrong?" as when a child might need Mummy or Daddy to get them out of a fix. They assume responsibility for errors and avoid confrontation.

Vata body types are usually have dry skin, dry hair, they are often thin build, but can put weight on usually around the middle. They have long faces, irregular teeth, smallish eyes, narrow lips, they can have long arms and or legs. The elements that they consist of are Ether and Air.

A Vata type can be summarised as having a variable and changeable character.

PITTA

Pitta consists of the elements of fire and water and is predominantly biased towards transformation. Fire and water govern the body's balance of chemical and transforming energies, including the digestion of both food and thought. In the mind, Pitta processes new data and draws conclusions.

PITTA HAS PARTICULAR QUALITIES, THESE ARE:

Light: Digestion, the processing of bulk and waste and activation of the body's natural cleansing activities are served by this Pitta quality, which helps create the balanced Pitta traits of freshness and alertness. In an unbalanced state, this can lead to ungroundedness. Pitta types suffer sore eyes when in very bright light and will usually be seen with sunglasses a lot of the time, but they also need enough good quality daylight to maintain a positive emotional outlook.

Hot: Pitta types may be physically hot and prone to perspiration, finding hot summer days difficult to cope with and have a tendency to sunburn. Despite this, they have lustrous skin and good complexions when in balance. Unfortunately, Pitta types are also prone to hot flushes and rashes when unbalanced. They are passionate with hot tempers and are quick to have heated exchanges with others. When balanced, this passion makes them good leaders. Heat is an essential component of digestion and most transformative processes, but because Pitta types have this natural heat, hot spicy food can aggravate them. Unbalanced Pitta heat can lead to inflammation, anger and hate.

Intense: Pitta types are often keenly intelligent, alert and highly focused and make good leaders, teachers, and advocates. They have intense relationships with equal measures of humour and argument. Their passions lead them to great lengths in support, defence, or promotion of what matters to them. They have intense arguments and won't concede easily. Intensity can be both active and passive, and Pitta types can be intensely roused and capable of moving mountains or intensely shut down, inactive and depressed. They feel the highs and lows of emotions, circumstances, and events deeply.

Medium: This quality epitomises the essence of a Pitta's balanced attributes. A balanced Pitta type can see both sides of a story. They eat well, neither gorging nor starving. They plan their days and work through an agenda without Vata airiness or Kapha lethargy, and they are in control of their lives. When unbalanced, this instinct to control becomes excessive, leading Pitta types to become overpowering and overdominant. They have balanced physiques regardless of height with well-proportioned limbs, necks and torsos, good muscle structure, and a capacity for endurance-based exercise. They have balanced facial features and clear, strong voices. Pitta hair can be fine and soft, fair, or reddish in colour, prone to premature greying but often lustrous and of good quality.

Sharp: Pitta types can have clear-cut features, such as a pointed chin or nose. They can be intelligent, have quick minds, sharp humour, grasp ideas easily and be articulate. Pitta types are 'on the ball'. They work quickly and act decisively, especially under duress, and a Pitta type is likely to be the one who takes charge in an emergency. Their conversation can be sharp and prickly in tone even when not aroused, and they can be irritable, jealous or aggressive. When unwell, they can experience sharp pain wherever their sickness is located, and this kind of pain, linked with the penetrating quality, is useful when diagnosing Pitta imbalances in any dosha.

Penetrating: Pitta types will have a penetrating gaze and the ability to get behind the smokescreens that many people put around themselves. They can see through hidden agendas but can also be judgemental in their comments. They are discriminating and able to organise ideas, arguments, and other people. They are quick learners and have good insight and memory. These qualities are also evident in less dramatic ways. Pitta's ability to penetrate often requires persistence, the capacity to ask searching questions and a willingness to dig behind the surface of appearances.

Pungent: This hottest and driest quality creates thirst and discomfort in Pitta types who are likely to need water in the middle of the night and, along with their natural heat, will seek out cold spots under the bedclothes. Pungency can be overpowering and forceful. In food, the pungent tastes are used sparingly because of their strength, and an unbalanced Pitta type can be 'over the top' exhibiting overbearing behaviour, often accompanied by pungent body odour. Balanced Pitta pungency has that edgy quality that snaps things into focus.

Acidic: Pitta qualities are specifically connected to digestive fire and transformation, processes that require acid as a key ingredient. Balance is critical, however, and unbalanced Pitta states create corrosive levels of acidity, leading to stomach pain, ulcers, biting, critical attitudes and cutting remarks. Acidity is essential for transformation but damaging when present in excess.

These qualities become manifested in a Pitta's behaviour, conversation, looks, sleep patterns, a tendency to perspire easily and reaction to hot food and weather.

In our bodies, Pitta is responsible for mental discrimination, visual perception, body temperature, skin and complexion, and digestion. All these qualities are found in all body types and are essential for normal life. We wouldn't function without the Pitta ability to transform and digest food, ideas and our perception. They are simply more obvious in Pitta types and become exaggerated when Pittas become unbalanced.

Pitta types are better suited to relaxation classes such as yoga, tai chi or qigong walking, swimming, meditation practice, moderate weight-based activities and natural environments. They are much less suited to aggressive, competitive games.

Balanced Pitta types make good decisions, are good leaders, are warm, bright, intelligent and have good digestion.

Unbalanced Pitta types are prone to anger, irritability and can be critical and judgemental. They can have skin problems and burning, heated complaints.

A typical Pitta stress response is, "What did you do wrong?"

Pitta body types are usually medium-built, with average proportions of legs and arms. Even fingers and toes can be well-developed and muscular. They often have fine hair that may be prematurely grey. They perspire easily, often with a keen odour, are passionate and have average levels of sleep.
A Pitta type will be prone to a hot temper and strong digestion.

Pitta types have sharp intellects and are direct and to the point. They prefer routine, have the courage of their conviction and make good teachers and leaders. They're good with money but like luxuries. They will be driven emotionally, physically and mentally.

A Pitta type can be summarised as being vigorous and fiery.

KAPHA

Kapha consists of the elements of earth and water and is predominantly biased towards stability. Kapha is concerned with earth and water and governs structure, bodily stability, lubrication and cell structure. In the mind, Kapha provides stability and the ability to grasp single thoughts.

KAPHA HAS PARTICULAR QUALITIES, THESE ARE:

Heavy: Kapha has substance. Kapha types have physical and emotional weight and the capacity to build and increase substance as a central aspect of the whole process of nutrition. Kapha types can have a serious approach to many issues, a willingness to embrace complexity and a 'heaviness' and depth that is reassuring to those around them. When unbalanced, this can lead to excess physical weight, lethargy, even laziness and heavy-handedness. They can become dull, often as a protective measure, since dulling the senses shields us from pain and difficulty, and they feel burdened and often bored.

Solid: Balanced Kapha types are enduring characters with reliable natures, 'salt of the earth' individuals around whom communities grow and flourish. They have sound judgement and sturdy self-belief. They are the strongest of the body types, with powerful core physiques, thick limbs and broad torsos, rounded features and quite large eyes and mouth, thick hair and thick skin that can be pale and cool. They are capable of hard physical effort. When unbalanced, this solidity turns to stubbornness, a 'lack of give' and a one-track-narrow-mindedness.

Stable: Kapha types are calm, steady and considerate individuals, patient, stable and slow to anger. There is an air of security around them. When balanced, they have reliable, unchanging personalities and possess a steady consistency around which other people are comfortable. They do not get agitated and make good listeners, the kind of people we can go to with a problem.

When unbalanced, they become inflexible and resistant to change, and this can lead to possessive and obsessive behaviour.

Cold: Kapha types are often physically or emotionally cool. They are affected by cool weather and withdraw into hibernation when possible. This coolness can help them when under pressure. When unbalanced, however, coolness becomes emotional detachment, denial, and withdrawal.

What might appear to be aloofness masks insecurity and a loss of that essential Kapha sense of self.

Smooth: In a positive, balanced state, this quality brings assuredness, evenness, and grace. Kapha types can be excellent dancers, exhibiting effortless movement. Kapha skin is smooth and free from blemishes, and their actions and speech are slow and rhythmic. When unbalanced, these qualities lead to slickness and a 'smooth talking' way of dealing with issues, to a slippery evasiveness and a tendency to hide feelings that can lead to passive-aggressive behaviour that masks an unwillingness to cooperate.

Slow: Kapha types are deliberate and measured and tend to be slow to learn something new but even slower to forget. They are visibly unhurried, and the Kapha type's slow, methodical natures allow them to resist pressure, avoiding wrong decisions and actions. They excel in logical analysis and take time to reach conclusions which are correspondingly well-founded. When unbalanced, this quality becomes excessive, and they almost grind to a halt, such is their slowness, to the point of sluggishness in any activity. They need long hours of sleep.

Structured: Balanced Kapha types are the building blocks of families, societies and businesses. They have the most solid constitutions of all the doshas. They are organised, ordered, reliable and stable at a deep, personal level. They can build structure and organisation into their personal and professional lives and help others to move to solid ground. When unbalanced, they become rigid and inflexible, unable to change direction or the basis of their thinking.

These qualities become manifested in a Kapha's behaviour and approach to most aspects of life, in their salt-of-the-earth character, their unwillingness to confront difficulty, their manner of speech and thought, their tendency to gain weight easily and their unwillingness to undertake major change.

In our bodies, Kapha is responsible for nurturing the nervous system, lubricating joints and the digestive tract and regulating water and fat. All body types require these Kapha functions to operate properly. The Kapha qualities of fluidity enable us to move with ease internally and in the external physical world. They are simply more evident in a Kapha type and become problematical when a Kapha is unbalanced.

Kapha types are better suited to heavy or explosive activity such as weightlifting, sprinting or any intense workout and are physically strong. They make good dancers, being light on their feet despite their heavier build.

Balanced Kapha types are steady, consistent, strong, and supportive.

Unbalanced Kapha types are prone to hoarding and can be lethargic, overweight, needy and lazy.

A typical Kapha stress response is, "I don't want to know."

Kapha body types are usually of heavier build with thick, full, and often oily hair, strong, solid legs and thick arms and shoulders. They gain weight easily and lose it with difficulty, sleep deeply and soundly and are slow to action.

Kapha types are easy-going, patient and prefer routine. They are usually devoted carers and are good with money and savings. A Kapha type is someone who is solid in structure, easily puts on weight and really dislikes any change.

A Kapha type can be summarised as being grounded and earthy.

It is worth restating that aspects of all three types are in each of us and that some are simply more dominant than others. The forces represented by each element are essential for the functioning of our bodies.

THE SIX TASTES

Conventional Western approaches to nutrition deal with proteins, carbohydrates and calories, but in Ayurveda, taste is the key issue, and there are six categories of taste that are critical to maintaining cellular health. All the tastes are necessary for our immunologic and spiritual functions. The essential tastes of nature, arising from the five elements, transmit vibrations that our bodies need to replenish our physical, emotional and spiritual rhythms. When these tastes are absent, we suffer.

Sweet is the dominant taste produced by the water and earth elements. The sweet taste increases bodily tissue, nurtures the body and relieves hunger.

Sour is formed from the earth and fire elements and helps digestion and the elimination of wastes.

Salty is useful in small quantities by all types. It helps to cleanse bodily tissues and activates digestion.

Pungent is formed from the elements of air and fire. It helps stimulate appetite and maintains metabolism and the balance of secretions in the body.

Bitter comes from the elements of air and space and can be used by all types in small quantities. Bitter detoxifies the blood, controls skin ailments and tones the organs.

Astringent is formed from the elements of earth and air and can be used in medicinal quantities by all types. The astringent principle helps to reduce bodily secretion and constricts bodily tissue.

VATA, PITTA, KAPHA TASTES

In Ayurveda, the six tastes are fundamental to understanding food and its effects on the body and mind. Each taste has specific qualities and effects on the doshas (Vata, Pitta, and Kapha) and contributes to overall balance and well-being.

THE SIX TASTES ARE:

Sweet taste is grounding, nourishing and calming, balances Vata and Pitta and aggravates Kapha. It promotes strength, satisfaction and stability in the body and mind. Sweet foods include grains, dairy, fruits, root vegetables and natural sweeteners like honey and maple syrup.

Sour taste stimulates digestion and increases salivation. It has a heating quality and can help balance excess Kapha and Vata. Sour foods include citrus fruits, vinegar, yoghurt, fermented foods and sour berries.

Salty taste enhances flavour and stimulates digestion. It has a grounding and hydrating effect, but excessive consumption can aggravate Pitta and Kapha. Salty foods include sea salt, seaweed, miso, soy sauce and salty cheeses.

Bitter taste detoxifies and purifies the body. It has a cooling and drying effect, helping to balance excess Pitta and Kapha. Bitter foods include leafy greens, bitter gourds, dandelion greens and turmeric.

Pungent taste stimulates metabolism and digestion, promoting circulation and warmth. It has a heating quality and can help balance excess Kapha and Vata. Pungent foods include chilli peppers, garlic, onions, ginger and black pepper.

Astringent taste has a drying and constricting effect, helping to tone tissues and reduce excess moisture in the body. It balances Pitta and Kapha and can be grounding for Vata. Astringent foods include green bananas, pomegranates, cranberries and most beans.

By incorporating all six tastes into meals, Ayurveda aims to create balanced and harmonious nutrition that supports optimal health and well-being. Each taste plays a vital role in nourishing the body, satisfying the senses and promoting holistic balance.

VATA TASTES:

Favour sweet, sour, salty

FOOD TYPE	FAVOUR – *TASTES FLUCTUATE*	AVOID
DAIRY	All dairy in moderation: buttermilk, cow's milk, hard cheese, soft cheese, ghee, goat's milk, goat's cheese, ice cream, sour cream, yoghurt	goat's milk, all powdered milk products
FRUITS	apricot, avocado, banana, berries, cherries, coconut, date, grapefruit, grape, kiwi, lemon, lime, mango, orange, peach, pineapple, plum (sweet), raisins (soaked), rhubarb (sweet), strawberry	apple, cranberry, dried fruits, pear, persimmon, pomegranate, prune, quince, watermelon
VEGETABLES	**Cooked vegetables**: artichoke, asparagus, beetroot, carrot, courgette, green bean (well-cooked), leek, okra, olives, onion, parsnip, potato (sweet), pumpkin, squash. **Salad**: radish, cucumber, watercress	frozen, dried or raw vegetables, artichoke, aubergine, broccoli, Brussels sprout, cabbage, cauliflower, capsicum, celery, fresh corn, leafy greens, lettuce, mushroom, raw onion, peas, potato (white), spinach, sprouts, tomato, turnip
BEANS/ LEGUMES/ NUTS/SEEDS	**Beans/legumes in moderation**: aduki, black lentils, mung, red lentils, soy cheese, soy milk, tofu, toor dhal **Nuts in moderation**: almond, Brazil, cashew, coconut, hazelnut, macadamia, peanut, pecan, pine, pistachio, walnut **Seeds**: flax, sesame, pumpkin, sunflower	**All other beans/legumes**: black bean, black-eyed pea, chana dhal, chickpea, kidney bean, brown lentils, lima, navy, pinto, soybean, split pea, tempeh, white **Seeds**: psyllium
GRAINS	oats (cooked), all rice, wheat, wild rice	barley, buckwheat, cold, dry puffed cereals, corn, granola, millet, oats (dry), oat bran, quinoa, rice cakes, rye, wheat bran
OILS	almond, corn, coconut, canola, mustard, olive, sesame, sunflower	animal fats, mixed vegetable oils
SPICES	ajwain, allspice, anise, asafoetida, basil, bay leaf, black pepper, caraway, cardamom, cayenne, cinnamon, cloves, coriander, cumin, dill, fennel, garlic (in moderation), ginger, mace, marjoram, mint, mustard seed, nutmeg, orange peel, oregano, paprika, parsley, peppermint, poppy seeds, rosemary, saffron, sage, spearmint, star anise, tamarind, tarragon, thyme, turmeric, vanilla	horseradish, fenugreek, neem leaves, raw garlic
SUMMARY	Favour warm, oily, heavy foods and sweet, sour and salty tastes. Use pungent, bitter and astringent tastes as accents, in moderation.	

PITTA TASTES:

Favour sweet, bitter, astringent

FOOD TYPE	FAVOUR – *TASTES FLUCTUATE*	AVOID
DAIRY	unsalted butter, cottage cheese, mild soft cheese, ghee, cow's milk, goat's milk, ice cream, yoghurt (diluted)	salted butter, hard cheese, feta cheese, sour cream, yoghurt
FRUITS	apple (sweet), apricot (sweet), avocado, berries (sweet), cherries (sweet), coconut, date, fig, grape (sweet), mango, melon, orange (sweet), pear, plum (sweet), pomegranate, prune, raisins, watermelon	apple (sour), apricot (sour), berries (sour), banana, cherries (sour), cranberry, grapefruit, kiwi, lemon, lime, orange (sour), papaya, peach, pineapple, plum (sour), rhubarb, strawberry
VEGETABLES	artichoke, asparagus, broccoli, Brussels sprout, cabbage, capsicum, cauliflower, corn (fresh), courgette, cucumber, celery, green bean, leafy greens, lettuce, mushroom, okra, parsnip, peas, potato (sweet and white), squash, sprouts, watercress	aubergine, beetroot, carrot, garlic, horseradish, leek, olives, onion (raw and cooked), pepper (hot), pumpkin, radish, spinach, tomato, turnip
BEANS/ LEGUMES/ NUTS/SEEDS	**Beans/legumes**: aduki, black beans, black-eyed pea, brown lentils, chana dhal, chickpea, kidney, lima, mung, navy, pinto, soybean, soy milk, soy cheese, split pea, toor dhal, tempeh, tofu, white **Nuts**: coconut **Seeds**: psyllium, pumpkin, sunflower	**Beans/legumes**: black and red lentils, toor dhal **Nuts**: almond, Brazil, cashew, macadamia, peanut, pecan, pine, pistachio, walnut **Seeds**: flax, sesame
GRAINS	barley, oats (cooked), rice (basmati and white), rice cakes, wheat, wheat bran	buckwheat, corn, millet, oats (dry and bran), quinoa, rice (brown), rye
OILS	avocado, coconut, olive, sunflower, sesame, soy, walnut (all in moderation)	almond, apricot, corn, sesame (dark)
SPICES	basil (fresh), black pepper (moderation), cardamom (moderation), cinnamon (moderation), coriander, cumin, dill, fennel, mint, neem leaves, orange peel (moderation), parsley (moderation), peppermint, saffron, spearmint, turmeric, vanilla	ajwain, allspice, anise, asafoetida, basil, bay leaf, caraway, cayenne, cloves, fenugreek, garlic, ginger, horseradish, mace, marjoram, mustard seed, nutmeg, onion, oregano, paprika, poppy seeds, rosemary, sage, star anise, tamarind, tarragon, thyme
SUMMARY	Favour cool food and liquids, sweet, bitter and astringent tastes and sour, salty and pungent tastes as accents.	

KAPHA TASTES:

Favour pungent, bitter, astringent

FOOD TYPE	FAVOUR – *TASTES FLUCTUATE*	AVOID
DAIRY	low or non-fat milk, low-fat yoghurt (diluted), ghee (in moderation), goat's milk	all other dairy, especially butter, cheese, full cream, ice cream, yoghurt (See beans for soy alternatives.)
FRUITS	apple, apricot, berries, cherries, cranberry, dried fruit, dried fig, peach, pear, persimmon, pomegranate, quince, raisins	avocado, banana, coconut, date, fresh fig, grapefruit, lemon, lime, melon, orange, mango, papaya, pineapple, plum, rhubarb, watermelon (grapes and kiwi in moderation)
VEGETABLES	artichoke (in moderation), aubergine, asparagus, beets, broccoli, Brussels sprout, cabbage, carrot, cauliflower, celery, corn (fresh), capsicum, garlic, green bean, horseradish, leafy greens, lettuce, mushroom, okra, onion, parsley, potato (white, in moderation), spinach, sprouts, summer squash, turnip, watercress	cucumber, courgette, olives, parsnip, sweet potato, pumpkin, tomato, squash, swede
BEANS/ LEGUMES/ NUTS/SEEDS	**Beans/legumes**: aduki, black beans, black-eyed peas, chana dhal, chickpea, lima, mung (in moderation), navy, pinto, red lentils, split pea–green or yellow, toor dhal, tofu (in moderation), white **Seeds**: flax, pumpkin, sunflower (in moderation)	**Beans/legumes:** black lentils, kidney, brown lentils, soybeans, soy milk (cold), soy cheese, soy flour, tempeh, cold tofu. **Nuts**: almonds, walnuts, Brazil nuts, cashew, coconut, macadamia, peanut, pecan, pine, pistachio **Seeds**: psyllium, sesame
GRAINS	barley, buckwheat, corn, cornmeal, millet, oats (dry), oat bran, quinoa, basmati rice (in moderation), rye, wheat bran, wheat (in moderation)	oats (cooked)
OILS	almond, canola, corn, mustard, sunflower (all in moderation)	avocado, coconut, olive, sesame, walnut
SPICES	ajwain, allspice, anise, asafoetida, basil, bay leaf, black pepper, caraway, cardamom, cayenne, cinnamon, cloves, coriander, cumin, dill, fennel (in moderation), fenugreek, garlic, ginger (dry), horseradish, mace, marjoram, mint, mustard seed, neem leaves, nutmeg, onion, orange peel, oregano, paprika, parsley, peppermint, poppy seed, rosemary, saffron, sage, spearmint, star anise, tarragon, thyme, turmeric, vanilla (in moderation)	salt, tamarind, mango powder
SUMMARY	Favour light, dry and warm foods and pungent, bitter and astringent tastes.	

BASIC STORE CUPBOARD

Grains – barley, buckwheat, bulgur wheat, couscous, millet, quinoa, oats, rice

Beans – aduki, butter beans, red kidney beans, black beans, haricot, mung (whole and split)

Peas – chickpeas, brown chickpeas, split green and yellow peas, dried whole green peas

Lentils – green, brown, puy, red

Tins/Jars/Cartons – tomatoes, sweetcorn, coconut milk, coconut water, plant-based milk, capers, mustard, tamarind paste, tamari, soy sauce

Fats/Oils – tahini, vegetable, olive, coconut, sesame, nuts, seeds

Flours/Baking – wholemeal, buckwheat, spelt, any other gluten-free alternatives of choice, baking powder, cacao powder, natural sugars, vanilla extract

Vinegars – apple cider vinegar, balsamic, liquid aminos

Dried Fruits – dates, figs, apricots, sultanas, raisins, etc.

Herbs/Spices – dried chilli flakes, cumin (ground and seeds), fennel seeds, coriander (ground and seeds), mint, thyme, rosemary, cinnamon, nutmeg, mixed spice, cardamom, clove, salt, pepper, asafoetida, bay leaf, cloves, fenugreek seeds, mustard seeds, saffron

Other – pasta, silken tofu, nutritional yeast flakes, vegetable stock, dried vegetables

This quote emphasises the interconnectedness of all living beings and underscores the importance of compassion and non-violence towards every creature. It reflects Gandhi's belief that true progress and greatness can only be achieved through practising Ahimsa in all aspects of life, including our treatment of animals.

The greatness of a nation and its moral progress can be judged by the way its animals are treated.

Gandhi

BREAKFASTS

Ayurveda considers breakfast to be an important meal of the day as it sets the tone for your digestion and energy levels.

Foods like cooked grains (such as rice or oatmeal), warm spiced milk, stewed fruits, nuts, seeds and herbal teas are often recommended.

Any cold food should be at room temperature and not straight from the fridge.

In Ayurveda, breakfast recommendations are based on each dosha. Here are some breakfast suggestions for each dosha.

Overall, regardless of dosha, Ayurveda emphasises the importance of eating mindfully in a calm environment and chewing food thoroughly to support proper digestion and assimilation of nutrients.

VATA QUALITIES – dryness, coldness and mobility. Warm, grounding foods will help balance Vata's erratic energy. Options may include cooked grains like oatmeal or quinoa, warm spiced milk, stewed fruits, ghee (clarified butter), nuts and seeds. Avoid cold or raw foods as they can aggravate Vata.

PITTA QUALITIES – heat, intensity and sharpness. Focus on cooling and soothing foods to balance Pitta's fiery nature. Options include sweet fruits like ripe mangoes or berries, coconut milk, soaked almonds and cooling herbal teas like peppermint or fennel. Avoid overly spicy or acidic foods as they irritate Pitta.

KAPHA QUALITIES – heaviness, coldness and stability. Focus on light and stimulating foods to energise Kapha's sluggishness. Options include warm, spicy foods like ginger tea, cooked vegetables with warming spices like black pepper or cinnamon, and light grains like quinoa or amaranth. Avoid heavy, oily or excessively sweet foods as they worsen Kapha imbalances.

AMAZING PROTEIN PURIFICATION SMOOTHIE

This is fantastic for your skin and amazing for lubricating your body whilst providing excellent protein and fibre to your purification process.

Coconut water has magnesium, phosphorus, calcium and potassium, a perfect blend to balance your electrolytes, which helps replenish minerals, salts and fluids.

Sunflower seeds are an excellent source of vitamin E and phytochemicals, which aid in anti-ageing.

Avocados are a superfood packed with healthy fats and proteins. Cooling for Pitta and grounding for Vata and use sparingly for Kapha.

INGREDIENTS

- 1 cup of room temperature coconut water* – a little cooler if it's summer
- ½ avocado
- 2 tbsp sunflower seeds
- 1 tbsp almond flour
- ½ banana
- 1 deseeded date to sweeten
- squeeze of lime juice

DIRECTIONS

Put all the ingredients in a blender and blitz until smooth.

**Ayurveda doesn't recommend chilled food as it dampens and weakens the digestive system.*

QUICK DELICIOUS BREAKFAST RICE

A comforting breakfast for all dosha types. It's great for Vata and Pitta types most days, but for Kapha types, make with half milk and half water.

Sona masoori rice is considered to be of much higher benefit than basmati. A medium grain rice meaning 'Golden Ivy'. It's fine to use your regular basmati, but you will see and taste the difference when you try sona masoori.

INGREDIENTS

- 1 cup of sona masoori rice already cooked or use poha rice (Poha is rice flakes and can have warm milk poured onto it without cooking.)
- 1 cup of milk of your choice
- ¼ cup of raisins
- ½ tsp cinnamon
- ½ tsp coriander powder
- ½ tsp ghee
- toasted sunflower seeds sliced almonds
- shredded unsweetened coconut

DIRECTIONS

1. Put all the ingredients in a small saucepan and mix well. Cook on medium heat until hot for about 5 minutes.
2. Share in two portions and add sunflower seeds, chopped almonds, and/or shredded coconut.

QUICK GOLDEN PORRIDGE & DATES

Quick Golden Porridge & Dates is a comforting and nourishing breakfast option that brings together the warmth of traditional oats infused with golden turmeric and the natural sweetness of juicy dates. This wholesome combination offers a delightful balance of flavours and textures, making it a perfect choice for starting your day on a nourishing note. With each spoonful, you'll experience the creamy richness of the porridge complemented by the subtle earthiness of turmeric, while the tender bites of dates add a delightful sweetness that leaves you feeling satisfied and energised.

Oats are naturally sweet and beneficial for Vata & Pitta dosha. They are also okay for Kapha if spices are added. You could also use the Kapha Masala Spice Mix on page 103 and sprinkle on top.

To be enjoyed hot or cold, this simple yet satisfying dish is sure to become a favourite in your morning routine.

DATES are sweet so **Kapha** types should be mindful of this. Increase the ginger and swap the dates for chopped apples.

INGREDIENTS

- 2 chopped dates
- 1 tsp turmeric
- ½ tsp fresh grated ginger
- 300ml of almond milk
- 1 handful of rolled oats
- 1 pinch of ground cinnamon

DIRECTIONS

1. Put all the ingredients into a saucepan and slowly bring to the boil.
2. Simmer until porridge is soft—about 5 minutes or so.
3. Serve with a sprinkle of cinnamon.

MILLET PORRIDGE

Millet is considered an ancient grain and holds the highest level of protein in the grain family, following amaranth and quinoa. It has been eaten and cultivated for centuries by the Tibetans.

High in iron and lecithin. Benefits the spleen, pancreas, stomach and gallbladder.

Helps keep cholesterol in check and reduces gallstones. Sweet, cooling, drying and salty in nature. Builds strong bones, tendons and ligaments. Good for athletes.

INGREDIENTS

- 1 cup of millet
- 1½ cup of water
- 1½ cup of milk of your choice. (We like to use raw organic milk, and plant-based milk is also good. You may need extra milk if the millet gets too thick during cooking.)
- ¼ tsp ground cinnamon
- ½ tsp vanilla essence
- 1 handful of chopped dates and raisins
- 1 spoon of barley syrup or honey to drizzle on top

DIRECTIONS

1. In a saucepan, add millet, water, milk, cinnamon, vanilla, dates and raisins. Bring to the boil, then reduce the heat to low, cover and simmer for 25 minutes without stirring.
2. If the liquid is not completely absorbed but not dry, check the millet is soft but not mushy. Cook a little longer if needed.
3. Serve in breakfast bowls and drizzle with the syrup or honey. You can add a small handful of coconut or blueberries. Blueberries are best for Kapha.

MILLET is best for **Kapha** types. **Vata** and **Pitta** types can eat millet in moderation adding lots of moisture for **Vata** and a spoonful of ghee for **Pitta.**

EASY WARM GRANOLA FOR ALL TYPES

This is a lovely change for Vata as they are always being told to have food that is warm and moist.

Oats are great for Vata & Pitta and fine for Kapha in a dry granola. Almonds are good, but almond oil is not great for Kapha. Ensure your almonds are peeled.

Adding a handful of nuts has a different effect. Walnuts are heating, dry, oily and heavy, so they are not so good for Kapha. Too many can create problems for Pitta.

INGREDIENTS

- 1 cup of rolled oats
- 1 small handful of chopped almonds
- 1 small handful of chopped walnuts
- 1 small handful of pecan nuts
- 1 small handful of sunflower seeds
- 2 tbsp shredded coconut
- 2 cardamom pods, slit at the end
- 1 large pinch of ground cinnamon – *more if you like it*
- 1 small handful of raisins
- 1 tbsp ground flaxseeds
- 150g organic vanilla yoghurt

DIRECTIONS

1. Soak your raisins in warm water to plump up and toss them in a towel to dry excess water.
2. In a large, heavy frying pan over a gentle heat, toast your oats, almonds, pecans and walnuts.
3. Stir constantly for 5 minutes, then add your sunflower seeds, coconut, cardamom pods and cinnamon powder.
4. Continue to stir for another 10 minutes.
5. Remove from heat and let it sit for a further 10 minutes.
6. Remove the cardamom pods, add the raisins and ground flax seeds.
7. Combine everything and mix the granola well.
8. Spoon over some room temperature vanilla yoghurt whilst it's all still warm.

DELICIOUS FRITTATA FOR ALL DOSHAS

Frittata is a really easy, nutritious and quick dish that can be adapted for all dosha types. It's great for a light lunch, or you can add extra vegetables or stuff a pitta bread with it for something more substantial.

INGREDIENTS

- ½ onion, chopped
- ½ yellow and red pepper, chopped
- 1 sweet tomato
- 8 small sun-dried tomatoes, chopped (halve this for Pitta)
- 6 well-beaten free-range eggs
- salt and pepper (reduce this for Pitta)
- 1 handful of mushrooms, chopped
- 1 handful of crumbly feta cheese (avoid this for Pitta and Kapha)

Not all Ayurvedic teachings choose to use eggs. We ensure that we get ours from a local neighbour who has chickens in her garden!

Cheese is considered difficult to digest for all doshas, so choose a light feta.

DIRECTIONS

1. In a large frying pan, fry the onion and peppers until translucent.
2. Add the fresh chopped tomato and chopped sundried tomato and cook for a few minutes, seasoning it with a little salt and pepper.
3. In a medium bowl, beat the eggs together with half of the crumbled cheese.
4. Pour this mixture over the vegetables in the frying pan and cook for a few minutes, allowing it to set.
5. Put the mushrooms and the rest of the crumbled cheese over the top.
6. Cook gently for 5-10 minutes until the egg has cooked through. You can lift the pan and keep pouring the raw egg underneath onto the hot pan.
7. Cook until it's set, then cut into triangles.
8. Serve with freshly cooked greens for Pitta, sweet potato chunks for Vata or salad for Kapha.

VATA - OK
PITTA - OK
KAPHA - OK

OIL FOR COOKING

VATA is best with sesame
PITTA is best with coconut oil
KAPHA is best with sunflower oil

TOFU

Tofu/soy is considered to be a food that's hard to digest according to Ayurveda, so it is something that we should consider for our digestive system. Times have moved on, and like all things Ayurvedic, we need to look at some new ways to help us accommodate foods that may upset our system. There are some good benefits of having tofu in our diets, so we always use herbs and spices to help with the assimilation of hard-to-digest foods.

SCRAMBLED TOFU & GREENS WITH GHEE

INGREDIENTS

- 1 tbsp ghee
- 1 clove garlic, minced 1 tsp soy sauce
- ½ or a little more of a pack of firm tofu
- ½ green pepper, diced 1 spring onion, diced
- ½ tsp ground ginger
- ½ tsp turmeric
- ½ tsp ground cumin
- Or use your own masala spice mix

DIRECTIONS

1. Drained your tofu and crushed it with a fork.
2. Sauté the spring onions and garlic in the oil for 3-5 minutes, until onions are slightly soft.
3. Add all the remaining ingredients except for salt and pepper.
4. Stirring frequently, cook for another 6-8 minutes until the vegetables are done and the tofu is lightly fried.
5. Add a dash of salt and pepper to taste. Eat with greens, salad or spinach.

You can use your specific **DOSHA MASALA SPICE MIX** in this recipe.

BAKED STUFFED APPLE BREAKFAST

Baked stuffed apples are a delightful dessert or snack that combines the natural sweetness of apples with a flavourful and aromatic filling. Each apple is carefully cored and filled with a delicious mixture of nuts, spices and sweeteners, creating a tantalising blend of textures and tastes. As they bake, the apples become tender and juicy, while the filling caramelises and infuses the fruit with irresistible flavour. Whether enjoyed warm from the oven or chilled, baked stuffed apples are a comforting treat, and cooked apples are great for the digestive system.

APPLES are great for **Pitta** and **Kapha** and suit **Vata** when cooked with spices like cinnamon, cardamom and ginger. They help relieve constipation and stewed apples are excellent for an upset tummy.

INGREDIENTS

- 30g walnuts, chopped 600ml non-dairy ice cream*
- 2 tbsp dark brown sugar
- 100g whole-grain cereal with dried fruit (We recommend muesli.)
- ½ lemon
- 60g butter, softened
- 4 large apples

DIRECTIONS

1. Heat the oven to Gas 7/425°F/220°C.
2. Trim the tops and scoop out the centre and seeds of each apple, then rub the edges of the trimmed fruit with the lemon.
3. In a medium bowl, combine the butter, cereal, sugar and walnuts.
4. Fill the apples with the cereal mixture.
5. Set the apples upright in muffin tins and bake for around 20 minutes until tender and bubbly. Transfer to serving dishes, top with ice cream and serve hot.

**Cold, particularly iced foods are not advocated for Ayurveda as they disrupt the digestive system, but now and then, they're delicious. Otherwise, add a non-dairy crème fraiche.*

BUCKWHEAT PANCAKE WITH FRUIT OR VEGETABLES

ACTIONS ON THE DOSHAS: balances **Vata** and **Kapha**, increases **Pitta** in excess.

You can do many things with crêpes by adding lots of sweet or savoury fillings. The crêpes themselves are full of goodness when made using buckwheat flour. You can eat them just with butter or ghee.

INGREDIENTS

- 1 cup of buckwheat flour*
- 1 free-range egg, or egg substitute
- ½ tsp baking powder
- ½ tsp energy flakes
- ½ - 1 cup of soya milk
- 1 tsp ghee

For a **sweet pancake**, add ½ mashed banana. Kapha use ½ grated apple.

For a **savoury pancake**, there is no need to add the fruit.

DIRECTIONS

1. In a bowl, combine the flour and baking powder. Add the soya milk a little at a time and beat it together until it becomes a thick, smooth batter. Add the banana/grated apple/energy flakes.
2. Melt the ghee in a heavy frying pan and drop round spoonfuls of batter onto the pan. When the batter starts to bubble, turn your pancakes over. We like to add a few blueberries or other berries at this stage. Broccoli florets or bean sprouts work too. Cook until golden brown.
3. Layer your pancakes with banana and berries or with Quorn sausages and scrambled egg. Ring the changes to make this your own breakfast, lunch or tea.
4. If sweet, serve with maple syrup.
5. If savoury, serve with crumbly cheese or tahini. Nutritious and delicious.

**Buckwheat is often thought of as a cereal, but it is actually a fruit seed.*

FOUNDATION JUICE

This Foundation Juice is used in all our purification programmes. It is wonderful for the body, skin and energy levels. It is rich in nutrients, and each ingredient contributes essential vitamins, minerals and antioxidants to the juice.

Apples provide fibre and vitamin C. Ginger offers anti-inflammatory and digestive benefits. Celery is rich in vitamins A, K, and C, and beetroot contains folate, potassium and manganese.

It's a good digestive aid as ginger and celery are known for their digestive properties. Ginger can help soothe the stomach and alleviate discomfort, while celery contains fibre that supports healthy digestion.

Ginger and beetroot both have anti-inflammatory properties that help reduce inflammation in the body, potentially benefiting conditions like arthritis or muscle soreness.

Beetroot is high in nitrates, which can help lower blood pressure and improve cardiovascular health. Also, the antioxidants in apples will contribute to heart health.

It is also a great purifying juice. It supports liver function and aids in the elimination of toxins from the body.

Overall, the Foundation Juice provides a refreshing and nourishing drink that supports overall health, digestion, inflammation reduction and hydration. However, individual responses to the juice may vary, so it's essential to incorporate it into a balanced diet.

INGREDIENTS

- 6 green apples
- thumb-sized piece of fresh ginger
- 1 pack of celery
- 3 raw beetroots with greens (if possible)

DIRECTIONS

It is best to be juiced, not blended.
Drink throughout the day.

Juicing and blending offer distinct benefits. Juicing extracts the liquid from fruits and vegetables, leaving behind pulp, resulting in a concentrated source of vitamins, minerals, and antioxidants. It's easy to digest and quickly absorbed by the body, making it an efficient way to consume nutrients.

On the other hand, blending retains the fibre from fruits and vegetables, promoting satiety, aiding digestion, and stabilising blood sugar levels. Blended drinks also tend to be thicker, which can help you feel fuller longer. Both methods can be valuable for increasing your intake of fruits and vegetables.

Choosing between them depends on what's required for each recipe.

PEA & MINT HUMMUS

Peas and mint are both cooling, sweet ingredients, making this hummus perfect for Pitta and fine for Vata. Kapha should avoid this unless they have been active from exercising or been on a long, hot walk during summer, so never say no.

You can add a good pinch of cumin and coriander if you like. This also helps improve digestion and adds extra flavour to the hummus.

INGREDIENTS

- 1½ cups of good quality frozen peas
- ½ clove of garlic
- 1 tbsp lemon juice
- ½ ripe avocado
- 2-3 sprigs fresh mint, using only the leaves
- cherry tomatoes

DIRECTIONS

1. Put the frozen peas in a bowl and cover with boiling water. Leave them to stand for about 5 minutes until they have defrosted.
2. Drain and blend on a high speed.
3. Add the garlic, lemon juice, avocado and mint leaves.
4. Season with a pinch of salt and continue to blend until smooth. Add a tablespoon of cold water if the mixture is too thick.
5. Add 1-2 cherry tomatoes chopped on top.
6. Serve as a dip with fresh vegetables, rice cakes or on gluten-free toast.

SOUPS

In Ayurveda, soups are valued for their nourishing and easy-to-digest qualities, especially during colder seasons. They are beneficial for the elderly and those with weak digestion.

Warm and well-spiced soups are always good. Ayurveda recommends warm foods to support digestion and balance the body. Generally, soups are ideally eaten warm, not hot, to avoid overheating the body. We love to add gentle spices like ginger, cumin, turmeric and black pepper to encourage digestion and add flavour.

Using seasonal and locally available ingredients is highly recommended in Ayurveda. This ensures that the body receives the nutrients it needs while aligning with the natural rhythms of the local environment.

Ayurveda likes to balance soups with vegetables, grains and beans to provide a variety of nutrients and support overall health.

Ayurveda reminds us to incorporate the six tastes as much as we can. This is easily achieved by adding spices.

Overall, Ayurvedic soups focus on incorporating wholesome ingredients, gentle spices and mindful preparation techniques to create nourishing and easily digestible meals that support overall health and well-being.

KIMBALAKE SOUP

Our most popular Ayurveda soup. Kimbalake is a sattvic dish. Foods that are considered sattvic are fresh, natural and unprocessed. Sattvic food nourishes the body, mind and spirit without causing any harm or imbalance. Sattvic foods typically include fruits, vegetables, whole grains, nuts, seeds, certain herbs and spices. Also, Ayurveda principles include dairy products from animals that are nurtured and cared for. Sattvic foods are believed to support physical health, mental clarity and spiritual development by fostering a sense of lightness, purity and vitality within the body.

INGREDIENTS

- 2 cups of sweet potatoes, chop to size according to how chunky you want the soup
- 1 cup of split red lentils
- 1 bunch of coriander, roughly chopped or 1 tbsp of dried coriander
- 1 tbsp cumin seed
- 1 tbsp fennel seed
- 1 tbsp vegetable stock (low salt bouillon)
- 1 tsp turmeric
- 1 tsp ginger
- 1 pint water
- ghee or oil for frying

Serve with:

- rice cake
- a bowl of green salad herbal tea

SWEET POTATOES can be kept for several months in a cool, dark place wrapped in brown paper bags.

DIRECTIONS

1. To make the masala paste, grind cumin and fennel seeds, ginger, turmeric, dry vegetable stock and salt in a pestle and mortar. Finely chop the coriander and put to one side (or if using ground coriander, add it into the pestle and mortar with the other spices). Add drops of water to the ground spice combination, mixing until it is a paste.
2. Fry this paste in a deep saucepan with a little vegetable ghee or olive oil, if you prefer. After a few minutes, add the chopped sweet potatoes and
3. red lentils, ensuring both are covered in the spice mix. Add the water, bring to the boil, then reduce to a simmer for 30-45 minutes. Scoop off any foam that appears.
4. You can continue adding more water until the soup is at the desired thickness.
5. Add your chopped coriander and serve.

CREAMY KALE & PUY LENTIL SOUP

This is a wonderful soup for a healthy lunch or a lighter evening meal and is perfect for all doshas.

INGREDIENTS

- 1 cup of puy lentils
- ½ cup of brown rice
- ½ medium-sized onion, finely chopped
- 4 tbsp olive oil
- 1 large bunch of kale or any other greens available
- 5 cups of water
- 1 or 2 cloves of garlic (High Pitta should only use 1.)
- 1 tsp cumin powder
- 1 tbsp vegetable bouillon
- ½ tsp curry powder
- salt and pepper to taste
- 1 tbsp tahini
- 1 tsp coconut oil
- 1 tbsp tamarind sauce or soy sauce

DIRECTIONS

1. Wash kale/greens and chop finely.
2. In a saucepan, heat the olive oil, add onions and cook until soft. Add the garlic and spices and blend well.
3. Then add the puy lentils and brown rice and stir well into the spice mix. Lastly, add the chopped kale/greens.
4. Add the water, bring it to the boil and simmer for about 45 minutes until the puy is cooked and soft.
5. While the soup is cooking, combine tahini, coconut oil and tamarind sauce until it is smooth and creamy. Add this to the soup mixture before serving and eat it as it is, or for a smoother consistency, puree it with a hand blender.

BROCCOLI, BEAN & PEA SOUP

One of our favourite soups. It is full of superfood goodness and tastes wonderful. This is a great immune-building soup. Broccoli aggravates Vata with its light, dry, bitter taste. Adding cream to the end of the soup and cooling with ghee will help with this.

VATA - aggravates
PITTA - OK
KAPHA - OK

INGREDIENTS

- 1 tbsp olive oil
  ¼ cup of spring onions, chopped
- 1 broccoli, cut into small florets
- 1 tbsp dried thyme
- ¼ tsp salt
- ¼ tsp ground black pepper
- 1 tbsp organic vegetable bouillon
- 1 cup of frozen peas
- ½ cup of mung beans, soaked for a couple of hours or overnight
- 1 good handful of clean, fresh spinach torn into little pieces
- cream or plant-based cream (optional garnish)

DIRECTIONS

1. Heat oil in a large saucepan over a medium-high heat until hot. Add the spring onion and cook for 3-5 minutes, stirring frequently.
2. Add broccoli, thyme, salt and pepper, and sauté for 5 more minutes. Cover your ingredients with water, add the bouillon and bring to the boil.
3. Once boiling, add the peas and mung beans and continue cooking for 15/20 minutes or until the beans and vegetables are tender. Add spinach at the end and cook for 5 more minutes or until the spinach is limp.
4. You can blend the soup, but we like to mash it with a potato masher and leave it with lots of texture. Add salt and pepper to taste.

RADISH & LEEK SOUP

This is a great soup and has more benefits than we can mention. Crunchy and succulent radishes are globally one of the most used vegetables in the form of salad.

RAW RADISH aggravates **Vata** & **Pitta.** Cooking them with potato makes them more acceptable.

INGREDIENTS

- 1 big handful of radishes, cut in half
- 2 large potatoes, peeled and cut into cubes (1 potato for Kapha)
- 2 large leeks, save a few rings to fry and add to the soup at the end (1 leek for Pitta)
- 1-2 tbsp organic vegetable bouillon
- 1 heaped tsp light miso paste
- 1 tbsp butter
- 1 cup of milk of your choice
- salt and pepper to taste
- rocket leaves to serve

DIRECTIONS

1. Wash and clean the leeks, then chop, leaving out the dark, rough tops.
2. Melt the butter in a saucepan, add the leeks (keeping some aside for frying later), radishes and potatoes and sauté for about 5 minutes. It's nice to just 'catch' the veg, not burn it—the extra flavour from a little burning is good.
3. Cover your ingredients completely with water, add the bouillon and simmer for about 45 minutes until everything is cooked through and soft.
4. In the meantime, fry the remaining leek rings until crispy. You will be adding them to the soup as a garnish later. Blend the soup, add the milk and season.
5. Reheat gently to serve. We like to add a small handful of rocket leaves on the top, with fried leek rings and slices of radish.

FRESH LEMON, CORIANDER & VEGETABLES

This is a lovely, fresh, tangy soup that is very moreish and really purifying.

VATA - OK
PITTA - OK
KAPHA - OK

INGREDIENTS

- 1 tbsp lemon juice
- 1 tsp grated lemon zest
- ¼ cup of finely chopped coriander leaves
- 1 tsp olive oil
- 1 tsp grated garlic
- 1 tsp finely chopped green chillies (1 tsp or less for Pitta)
- ¼ cup of finely chopped onions
- ¼ cup of finely chopped/shredded cabbage/kale
- ¼ cup of finely chopped/shredded carrots
- 1 cup of organic vegetable bouillon stock
- salt to taste

DIRECTIONS

1. Heat the oil in a saucepan, add the garlic, green chillies and sauté on a medium heat for a few seconds—smell the fragrance.
2. Add the onions and gently fry on a medium heat for a couple of minutes.
3. Now add the grated cabbage/kale and grated carrots. Fry on a medium heat for a further 2 minutes.
4. Pour in the bouillon stock, lemon juice, lemon zest and salt. Stir completely and simmer for about 15 minutes or so until the vegetables are softer but not mushy. Keep stirring occasionally.
5. Finish by adding the coriander leaves. Cook for another minute and immediately serve while hot.

BUTTERNUT SQUASH & CHILLI BROTH

Butternut squash is the most potent winter vegetable, full of antioxidants to keep your colds away, as well as other wonderful components.

VATA – OK
PITTA – reduce chilli if you are high Pitta
KAPHA – in moderation

INGREDIENTS

- 1 peeled squash or sweet potato
- 1 de-seeded red chilli pepper, chopped
- 1 tsp vegetable bouillon (We use Marigold Swiss Bouillon.)
- 1 small onion, chopped
- 1 tsp ground cumin seeds
- 1 tsp ghee or sunflower oil
- almond milk
- squeeze of lime or lemon juice
- crème fraiche or yoghurt (for garnish)

DIRECTIONS

1. Chop the squash, add to a saucepan, cover with water with the bouillon and bring to the boil. In the meantime, gently fry the chopped chilli, chopped onion and ground cumin seeds.
2. Once the onion is soft, add to the pan of squash and cook until the squash is soft.
3. Either mash or blend, adding some almond milk until you reach your desired thickness. At the end, squeeze in your lemon or lime juice.
4. Add a teaspoon of your garnish, then serve. Delicious.

BUTTERNUT SQUASH, CARROT & APPLE

A warming, purifying soup which is packed full of healthy nutrients.

INGREDIENTS

- 1 small butternut squash or sweet potato
- 3 carrots
- 1 clove garlic, crushed
- ½ thumb size fresh ginger, peeled and grated
- 4-5 cups vegetable stock
- 1 tbsp ghee
- 1 apple, peeled and cored
- 1 tsp cinnamon
- salt and pepper

DIRECTIONS

1. Preheat oven to Gas 7/425°F/220°C.
2. Cut your butternut squash or sweet potato, if using, in half, lengthwise. Remove seeds. Brush with ghee. Add salt and pepper, and sprinkle with a little cinnamon.
3. Peel and cut the carrots into slices.
4. Place the butternut squash, carrots and crushed garlic on a greased baking sheet and bake until soft for 45-50 minutes, depending on the size of your vegetables—keep an eye on them.
5. Remove the squash from the oven and peel the skin away.
6. In a large saucepan, add the chopped apples and remaining ingredients and cover with vegetable stock. Cook for 5 minutes or until the apples are soft.
7. Then, transfer the whole mixture into a blender and blitz until smooth. Add ginger, cinnamon and cardamom and reheat in the same large saucepan or for 5 minutes or so to flavour the soup. Very cleansing and nourishing!

MUNG BEAN SOUP

A favourite amongst students. Mung Bean Soup is a nutritious and comforting dish made from whole green mung beans. It's often cooked with various vegetables and spices. This one is a simple, healing, hearty basic recipe with a lovely texture and earthy flavour, making it a popular choice for purification practices.

This soup is highly nutritious and naturally cleanses the body, including the liver, gallbladder and vascular system of any Ama (undigested toxins).

VATA - OK
PITTA - OK
KAPHA - OK

INGREDIENTS

- 1 mug of soaked green mung beans
- 4 mugs of water
- 1 tsp turmeric
- 2-3 tsp grated ginger
- 1 pinch of asafoetida or hing
- 1 tsp each of cumin seeds, ground coriander and fennel seeds
- 1 tbsp vegetable bouillon
- 2-3 tbsp freshly squeezed lemon juice
- 1 tsp ghee or coconut oil
- salt and pepper
- 1 handful of fresh coriander, finely chopped

DIRECTIONS

1. Wash the mung beans thoroughly and soak overnight or for at least four hours. Drain the soaked beans and add them to a large saucepan with the water and turmeric. Simmer for about 30 minutes until the beans are soft and falling apart. You can add more water if needed.
2. Whilst it is cooking, fry the remaining herbs (not the fresh coriander) and spices for 2 minutes in the oil of your choice. Once aromatic, pour the whole spice mixture into the cooked beans.
3. At the very end, add the lemon juice, some fresh coriander and stir into the soup.

SIMPLE, MOREISH PEA & MINT SOUP

Pea and mint together are a classic flavour pairing that complements each other really well. This soup has the sweet, earthy taste of the peas and is enhanced by the refreshing, bright notes of mint. Together, they create a harmonious balance of flavours that's fresh and satisfying.

INGREDIENTS

- 1 small bag of frozen, fresh or dried peas
- 1 tbsp vegetable bouillon
- 1 small handful of chopped fresh
- 1 tbsp sliced almonds
- 1 tbsp sunflower seeds
- 1 tbsp pine nuts
- mint (save some for garnish)
- a few chopped mint leaves.

DIRECTIONS

1. Put the peas into a saucepan and cover with hot water. Bring to the boil. If using dried peas, follow the packet instructions. Add a handful of mint (save some for garnish) and the bouillon. Cook for 15 minutes until peas are cooked through and soft.
2. Pour into a blender and blitz until smooth. Add extra water if it is too thick.
3. Serve with seeds, nuts and and a few chopped mint leaves.

VATA – OK
PITTA – OK
KAPHA – As it's cooling and sweet it's not a great one for **Kapha** so eat in moderation and add Kapha Masala Spice Mix on p.103

BROCCOLI & ALMOND SOUP

This is not a common pairing, but it came about from experimenting and has become a firm favourite. This combination is nutty with a sweet, earthy flavour of broccoli. Made into a creamy soup, the combination of broccoli and almonds adds depth and complexity to the soup.

VATA - OK
PITTA - OK
KAPHA - OK

INGREDIENTS

- 1 small broccoli broken into florets (save some for garnish)
- 1 small onion, chopped
- 1 clove of garlic, grated
- ½ cup of almond flour
- 1 tsp bouillon

DIRECTIONS

1. In a large saucepan, add chopped broccoli, onion and garlic.
2. Cover with water and bring to the boil.
3. Add the bouillon and simmer for 15-20 minutes, then add the almond flour and
4. Simmer for a further 10-15 minutes.
5. Either pour into a blender or use a stick blender in the pan to make a smooth mixture.

AYURVEDIC SIMPLE VEGETABLE SOUP

A simple vegetable soup recipe incorporating sweet potato, red pepper, squash, carrot, parsnip and onion. This soup incorporates a variety of colourful vegetables, providing a range of nutrients and flavours.

Suitable for all doshas but **Kapha** should be careful of too much sweetness.

INGREDIENTS

- 1 sweet potato, peeled and diced
- 1 red pepper, diced
- 1 small squash (such as butternut or acorn), peeled, seeded and diced
- 1 carrot, peeled and diced
- 1 parsnip, peeled and diced
- 1 onion, finely chopped
- 4 cups bouillon
- 1 tbsp ghee or coconut oil
- 1 tsp ground cumin
- 1 tsp ground coriander
- ½ tsp turmeric powder
- salt and pepper
- fresh coriander or parsley

DIRECTIONS

1. Wash, peel and dice all the vegetables.
2. In a large pot, heat the ghee or coconut oil over a medium heat. Add chopped onion and sauté until translucent.
3. Add ground cumin, ground coriander, turmeric powder, salt and pepper to the pot. Stir well to coat the onions with the spices.
4. Add diced sweet potato, red pepper, squash, carrot and parsnip to the pot. Stir to combine with the spices and onions. Pour the vegetable broth into the pot, ensuring that the vegetables are fully submerged. Bring the soup to the boil, then reduce the heat to low and let it simmer for about 20-25 minutes or until the vegetables are tender.
5. For a creamier texture, you can blend a portion of the soup and then return it to the pot.

COURGETTE & TARRAGON SOUP

Courgette and tarragon make a wonderful flavour pairing that complements each other really well. The mildness of courgette offers a subtle, slightly sweet flavour. With its delicate texture, courgettes are a great cleansing base for the tarragon taste to shine. The distinctive and unique flavour of tarragon is often described as slightly liquorice-like, with hints of pepper and citrus. It adds a refreshing and aromatic dimension to this soup. Courgette & Tarragon Soup is suitable for all three doshas—Vata, Pitta and Kapha. It is best for Kapha during the hotter seasons.

INGREDIENTS

- 1 onion, chopped
- 1 tbsp olive oil
- 6 medium courgettes, chopped
- 1 tbsp fresh tarragon or 1 tbsp dried
- 1 cup of soya milk
- 1 tsp organic bouillon
- 1 cup of water

DIRECTIONS

1. Fry the onion gently until translucent, not brown. Add the chopped courgettes and herbs and gently fry for 2-4 minutes.
2. Add the remaining ingredients to the pan and bring gently to the boil for 15-20 minutes. Blend into a smooth soup. Serve with greens and a rice cracker.

DETOX SOUP

Detox Soup is a nourishing and cleansing dish that offers a comforting way to reset and rejuvenate the body. Packed with vibrant vegetables, herbs and spices, each spoonful of this flavourful soup delivers a burst of nutrients and antioxidants. The combination of wholesome ingredients helps to support the body's natural detoxification processes, promoting overall health and vitality. Whether enjoyed as a light meal or a soothing snack, Detox Soup provides a nourishing option to help you feel refreshed and revitalized from the inside out.

INGREDIENTS

- 2 - 3 cups water
- 1 tsp organic vegetable bouillon (We use Marigold.)
- 1 cup of leafy greens, washed and torn, e.g. spinach, kale, rainbow chard
- 1 cup of chopped carrots
- ½ apple, chopped
- 1 small handful of yellow split mung beans
- 1 clove garlic, grated
- 1 tbsp grated fresh ginger
- ½ tsp each of turmeric, ground cumin and ground coriander
- 1 tbsp tahini
- 1 tbsp freshly chopped coriander
- 1 tbsp fresh chopped parsley
- 1 tbsp flaxseed oil
- sesame seeds – optional
- 1 tbsp sesame seeds

DIRECTIONS

1. In a saucepan, add the water, bouillon, greens, carrots, apple, lentils, garlic, ginger and spices. Cover and bring to the boil and then let it simmer for 30-45 minutes.
2. When it's ready, blend it and add more water depending on your desired thickness. Add a splash of tahini into the soup, then stir in the fresh coriander, parsley and a drizzle of flax oil. You can also sprinkle sesame seeds on top.

MEALS

According to Ayurveda, main meals should be balanced, nourishing and considered towards individual doshas for optimal health and well-being.

Ayurveda emphasises a balanced meal that includes a variety of the six tastes of Ayurveda. This helps to satisfy and support digestion, ensuring the body receives a wide range of nutrients.

Choose seasonal and fresh ingredients whenever possible. Seasonal foods are believed to be more aligned with nature's rhythms and offer the nutrients needed to support the body during different times of the year.

Incorporate digestive spices like ginger, cumin, coriander, turmeric and fennel into main meals. These spices help improve digestion, enhance flavour and balance the doshas.

Breathe and take the time to prepare meals mindfully, bringing positive energy and intention.

MUNG BEAN WITH COCONUT

SATTVIC - good for all body types

This is one of my favourite dishes. I make it at nearly all of my workshops—everyone loves it!

INGREDIENTS

- 1 cup of whole green mung beans (mung beans are considered tridoshic and fine for all doshas)
- salt and pepper
- ½ tsp turmeric
- 1 tsp ground fennel seeds
- 6 cups water
- 1 tbsp ghee
- 1 small onion, finely chopped
- 1 small carrot, peeled and diced
- 1 clove garlic, finely chopped
- 1-inch piece of ginger, peeled and finely chopped
- 1 tsp garam masala
- ½ tsp chilli flakes (I rarely add these, being a Pitta type)
- 2-3 small tomatoes, chopped*
- 1 cup of light coconut milk
- 1 tbsp lime juice
- yoghurt (not Kapha)

**Tomatoes are aggravating for all doshas so are not used in many recipes as they are strongly acidic and sour. Use them sparingly.*

DIRECTIONS

1. There is no need to soak mung beans, but we always like to; it ensures that the beans are beautifully soft. After soaking for a couple of hours, wash the mung beans thoroughly. Put them in a large pot with 3 cups of water, salt, turmeric and fennel seeds. Bring to the boil. Keep covered and simmer for about 45 minutes until the beans are soft. Skim off any foam that rises to the surface.
2. Heat the ghee in a medium-sized pot or large saucepan and add the onions, carrots, garlic and ginger. Sauté over a low-medium heat. Add the chilli flakes and garam masala. Cook slowly until the vegetables are soft. Season lightly with a pinch of salt and set aside until the mung beans are done.
3. Combine the mung beans, vegetables, 3 cups of water and tomatoes. Simmer for about 15 minutes. Let the soup thicken and the flavours blend. Stir in coconut milk and the lime juice just at the end of cooking. When you have served the soup, add a dollop of yoghurt. Kapha should avoid the yoghurt.

THE AMAZING ENERGY KALE WITH CHICKPEAS

Kale is so filled with goodness; it's hard to believe. This is what Ayurveda says about kale. Kale is a blood cleanser and one of the best cancer-fighting vegetables. Rich in vitamins A and C, riboflavin, niacin, calcium, magnesium, iron, sulphur, sodium, potassium and chlorophyll.

VATA – in moderation
PITTA – OK
KAPHA – OK

INGREDIENTS

- 1 bunch of kale, thick stems and ribs removed, leaves coarsely chopped
- 2 tbsp extra-virgin olive oil
- salt
- 1 handful of energy flakes
- 1 small tin of chickpeas, drained
- 1 tbsp tahini

DIRECTIONS

1. Preheat the oven to Gas 2/300°F/150°C.
2. In a large bowl, toss the kale with the olive oil, energy flakes and a few pinches of salt. Spread the kale out onto a large baking sheet. Bake until a little crispy on the edges but still tender, 8-10 minutes. Make sure you keep an eye on it, so it doesn't burn.
3. Remove the kale from the oven and toss with the tahini and chickpeas. Eat from a bowl, but we love this piled onto other dishes.

KALE is cooling for **Pitta** so a good alternative to spinach in other recipes.

WARM BEETROOT SALAD WITH WALNUTS & SPINACH

This is one of my favourite dishes, a nourishing and flavourful dish that not only satisfies the taste buds but also provides great health benefits. It's a staple in many of my Ayurvedic purification programmes due to its simplicity, nutrient density and ease of preparation.

BEETROOT is sweet and **Kapha** aggravating, but spinach will help to counter the effects.

INGREDIENTS

- 1 cooked beetroot, cut into chunks
- ¼ tsp cumin
- ¼ tsp ground coriander
- ¼ tsp ground turmeric
- 1 handful of halved walnuts.
- 1 bag of spinach – rocket also works
- fresh chives, chopped
- 1 tsp olive oil
- slithers of any cheese as an added extra protein – *optional*

DIRECTIONS

1. In a frying pan, add a teaspoon of olive oil and lightly fry the cumin, ground coriander and turmeric. Toss in the beetroot chunks and fry for a minute or two.
2. Place spinach on a plate, arrange beets on top with walnuts, and sprinkle with chives and cheese if using. Finish with a drizzle of olive oil.

VATA – OK
PITTA – reduce spinach or add kale
KAPHA – in moderation

SO EASY GORGEOUS COCONUT CURRY

Ayurveda sees coconut as cooling and very effective in curing hyperacidity with its Pitta pacifying quality. It is good for removing toxins from the body and purifying the digestive system. Coconut balances acid levels and cools the digestive system. So there is lots of goodness in this dish.

Remember, if you are a high **Pitta** you should only eat this on occasion, but this has a good balance of spices for all types.

INGREDIENTS

- 1 bunch of spring onions, chopped
- 400g tin coconut milk
- 1 small butternut squash, peeled and chopped
- 1 parsnip, peeled and chopped
- ½ of a cauliflower cut into small florets
- 1 small bag of chopped cashew nuts, unsalted

Spices

1 tsp each of:

- turmeric
- tamarind paste
- coconut oil for frying
- black mustard seeds
- cumin seeds
- 1 clove of garlic chopped

DIRECTIONS

1. Put all the spices and oil into a frying pan and gently cook for about 2 minutes until fragrant. Let the mustard seeds pop, then add the chopped spring onions and cook for a few minutes until soft.
2. Stir in the coconut milk and add the chopped vegetables. Turn the heat low and simmer for 15-20 minutes. When the vegetables are cooked, serve on a bed of basmati rice and sprinkle the cashew nuts on top.

HERBY WHITE BEAN STEW

This comforting, steaming bowl of Herby White Bean Stew provides warmth and nourishment. With the creamy texture of the haricot beans, it's perfectly complemented by the variety of vegetables and herbs. If you have fresh herbs like rosemary and thyme in your garden, add a sprig of each to the pot. Haricot beans are perfect for Pitta, so you can eat more in this dish than Vata.

VATA - in moderation
PITTA - OK
KAPHA - moderation

INGREDIENTS

- 1 large tin of haricot beans
- 4 cups of vegetable stock
- 2 bay leaves
- 1 tsp ghee/oil
- ½ cup of chopped leeks
- 1 cup of chopped red and green bell pepper
- ½ tsp black pepper
- 5 tsp Vata, Pitta or Kapha Masala Spice Mix, *see pages* 101-103
- 2 tbsp soy sauce
- 2 cups of carrots, cut into small cubes
- 1 cup of courgettes, cut into small cubes
- 1 cup of washed spinach, coarsely torn
- 3 sweet ripe tomatoes, skinned and pulped
- squeeze of lime juice
- chopped fresh parsley

DIRECTIONS

1. Heat the ghee/oil in a frying pan over a low heat. Add the leeks, bell peppers, black pepper, masala mix and soy sauce. Cook for about 3 minutes until the leeks are translucent. Add the carrots and haricot beans and coat in the herb mix.
2. Transfer everything except the lime juice and parsley, including the courgettes, spinach and tomato into a large cooking pot. Cover with the stock and bring to the boil. Add more stock if necessary. The contents need to be fully covered.
3. Reduce and simmer for about 15 minutes until the carrots are cooked through. We like to turn the pan off and leave it covered for at least an hour to really meld in the wonderful flavours. Before serving, add the lime juice and parsley.

MUSHROOM, CASHEW NUT & BARLEY RISOTTO

Mushrooms should always be cooked. According to Ayurveda, they are very difficult to digest when raw. Light and dry would be aggravating for Vata but with added cashews, it helps. Barley is also cool and dry, so Vata should use rice or quinoa.

INGREDIENTS

- 4-6 fresh medium mushrooms of your choice, sliced
- 1 small onion, chopped
- 1 garlic clove, chopped
- 2 - 3 cups vegetable bouillon
- 1 tsp coconut oil
- 1 handful of cashew nuts, chopped
- 1 cup of pearl barley
- soy sauce

DIRECTIONS

1. Cook the pearl barley in the vegetable bouillon and simmer until the barley absorbs the water. Whilst it's cooking, prepare the other ingredients.
2. Gently fry all the other ingredients in the coconut oil for a few minutes until the onion is soft. When the barley is just al dente, fold in your fried ingredients.
3. Serve immediately with a drizzle of soy sauce and the chopped cashew nuts.

VATA – avoid or in moderation
PITTA – OK
KAPHA – in moderation

QUICK & EASY STIR-FRY WITH TURMERIC

Quick and easy stir-fry vegetables are a go-to solution for busy weeknights or whenever you need a healthy and satisfying meal in a hurry. With a colourful array of fresh vegetables tossed together in a hot pan with flavourful sauces and spices, this dish bursts with vibrant flavours and textures. Whether it's crunchy bell peppers, crisp snap peas, or tender broccoli florets, each bite offers a delicious medley of tastes that will leave you feeling satisfied and nourished. Slice up any vegetables in your store very thinly. This is so that they can cook through quickly when you stir-fry them.

INGREDIENTS

- 2 tbsp ghee
- 1 tsp turmeric
- salt and pepper
- 2 tbsp water

Vegetables you can use:

- coloured peppers
- courgettes
- red cabbage
- carrots
- broccoli
- spinach
- spring onions

DIRECTIONS

1. Heat the ghee and water in a wok or large frying pan. Add the turmeric and seasoning. Toss in the finely sliced vegetables in the spiced oil and water. Cover and cook, stirring often, for about 10 minutes or so until the vegetables are cooked.

HEALTHY TOFU – FRIED RICE & VEGETABLES

This is a delicious, easy and nourishing evening meal. However, Tofu is heavy and cold, and some say it is not easy to digest. The extra spices help with digestion.

VATA - OK
PITTA - OK
KAPHA - Tofu can aggravate **Kapha** because of its heavy, cold nature.

INGREDIENTS

- 1/2 pack of tofu, cut into small cubes
- handful each of carrots, broccoli, cabbage, courgettes, etc., all cut up small
- 1 cup of *cooked* basmati rice
- 1 tsp ghee
- ½ tsp cumin seeds
- ½ tsp turmeric
- ½ tsp ground coriander
- ½ tsp grated fresh ginger
- ½ tsp fennel seeds - if you like the taste

DIRECTIONS

1. Chop and steam (boil if you do not have a steamer) the vegetables for about 15 minutes until cooked.
2. Heat a teaspoon of ghee in a frying pan. Add the tofu and spices, and gently fry for a few minutes until the tofu is coated and smells great.
3. Add the vegetables and the cooked rice to the frying pan. Toss all ingredients until they are fully coated in spices and ghee.

EASY DELICIOUS DHAL

Red lentils are sweet, astringent and cooling. They are balancing for all doshas when the spices and oil are included. See notes in the recipe.

VATA - OK
PITTA - OK, but reduce ginger and no chilli flakes
KAPHA - OK, but reduce ghee

INGREDIENTS

- 1 cup of well-rinsed red lentils
- 2-inch piece of fresh ginger, grated (reduce for Pitta)
- 2 bay leaves
- 1 cinnamon stick
- 2 tbsp ghee (reduce for Kapha)
- 1 onion, chopped.
- 1 clove of garlic, chopped
- 2 tsp turmeric
- 1 tsp cumin
- ½ tsp chilli flakes (none for Pitta)
- 2 tbsp lemon juice
- salt to taste

DIRECTIONS

1. Place red lentils, grated ginger, bay leaves and cinnamon stick in a large saucepan with 3 cups of cold water. Bring to the boil, then reduce the heat to medium and simmer, stirring for 10-12 minutes to prevent sticking. Remove the bay leaves and cinnamon stick.
2. Heat the ghee in a large frying pan over a medium-high heat. Add the chopped onion and cook for 3 minutes. Stir in the chopped garlic, turmeric, cumin and chilli flakes and cook for a further minute or until it smells delicious. Stir in the lemon juice and season to taste with salt. Add this spice mix to the lentils and water. Mix thoroughly and cook for a further 5 minutes or so, stirring to avoid sticking to the pan.
3. Serve with a selection of cooked vegetables like cauliflower, broccoli or green salad. Delicious! Try and resist the temptation of eating with bread!

SHEPHERD'S PIE – VEDA STYLE

This is such an easy, nutritious dish with layers of hearty vegetables seasoned with warming spices like cumin and coriander — a rich, tasty plate of goodness. On top is a blanket of creamy mashed sweet potatoes baked to perfection. Shepherd's Pie - Veda style is a comforting and nourishing dish.

INGREDIENTS

- 3-4 medium sweet potatoes
- a little milk for the mash
- 1 tbsp ghee
- ¼ tsp cumin
- ¼ tsp coriander
- 3 finger pinch of salt
- 4 cups of steamed vegetables, such as broccoli, carrots, celery, onions, courgette, etc.
- ½ cup of water from steamed vegetables
- 1 tsp vegetable bouillon
- 1 tsp tamari
- grated cheese of your choice for topping

DIRECTIONS

1. Preheat the oven to Gas 4/350°F/180°C.
2. Boil the potatoes (you can peel your potatoes, which will make digestion easier, or leave the skins on for more roughage). Once cooked, mash the potatoes with the milk to make them fluffy. Chop all the vegetables and steam/boil until almost cooked.
3. Add the bouillon, tamari and just enough water to cover the vegetables. Stir to mix.
4. Put the vegetable mix into an ovenproof dish, cover it with the mashed potatoes, and sprinkle it with cheese. Cook in the oven for about 30 minutes until the top is golden.
5. We suggest serving with red cabbage.

In the colder months, the digestive system steps up a notch. This is good for all types. However, **Kapha** should eat smaller portions.

QUINOA & ORANGE BOWL

Quinoa and orange make a delicious Ayurvedic combination, balancing flavours and providing a nourishing blend of nutrients. Quinoa is a protein-rich grain that is considered light and easy to digest, making it suitable for all doshas. It is also known for its grounding properties and ability to provide sustained energy throughout the day. Oranges are sweet and sour, offering a burst of vitamin C and antioxidants. In Ayurveda, oranges are considered cooling and refreshing, helping to balance Pitta dosha and support digestion. Combined, quinoa and oranges create a harmonious dish that is both satisfying and rejuvenating, making it a perfect addition to a balanced Ayurvedic diet.

INGREDIENTS

- 1 cup of cooked quinoa, warm or cooled
- 3 small oranges, or satsumas or sliced large orange (reserve some segments/slices to serve)
- dozen golden sultanas
- 1 celery stalk, finely chopped
- 1 handful of chopped walnuts
- 1 spring onion, sliced small
- 1 small handful of chopped parsley
- 1 handful of your favourite leaves

For the dressing:

- use the juice from oranges
- squeeze of lemon juice
- small piece of ginger, grated
- drizzle of olive oil

DIRECTIONS

1. Toss all the ingredients together
2. Add all the dressing ingredients to a jar and shake. Add dressing on top.
3. Serve in bowls.

KICHADI

Kichadi is tridoshic, which is good for all types. It is considered one of the most auspicious meals in Ayurveda. This quick, basic recipe requires two main components. The marriage between the grain and the bean is one of the oldest and traditional Ayurveda healing recipes. This particular one has been adapted with a tasty mix of spices.

RICE AND BEAN/LENTIL

Basmati rice is considered the most versatile rice in Ayurveda, although some ancient texts refer to 'Sona Masoori' as the very best light-medium grain white rice for quality results. It's always good to try both and see which you prefer.

LEGUMES, BEANS, PEAS

For Vata - mung dhal , split or whole

For Pitta- mung dhal , split or whole

For Kapha- red lentils, split peas green or yellow

OILS

For Vata - almond, sesame, sunflower, ghee

For Pitta - coconut, soy, sunflower, ghee

For Kapha - corn, sunflower, ghee

VEGETABLES

For Vata - onions

For Pitta - leek (if wanted)

For Kapha - onions

SPICES

For Vata - coriander, cardamom, cumin, black pepper, cloves, cinnamon, garlic (less)

For Pitta - cumin, cloves (less), cardamom (less), coriander, cinnamon, fennel, saffron, black pepper (less)

For Kapha - coriander, cardamom, cumin, black pepper, cloves, cinnamon, garlic

All doshas - vegetable stock

BASIC QUICK FOUNDATION KICHADI

Basmati rice and yellow split mung bean/dal (The yellow split mung beans do not need soaking.)

Oils – ghee or another preferred choice

Spices – coriander, cardamom, cumin, Organic (salt-free preferred) vegetable bouillon (We always use Marigold Bouillon.)

VATA - OK
PITTA - OK
KAPHA - OK

INGREDIENTS

- 1 tsp oil
- 1 tsp vegetable bouillon
- 1 cup of basmati rice
- 1 cup of split mung beans 6 cups of water

Spices

- 1 tbsp coriander seeds
- 1 tbsp cardamom pods, about six
- 1 tbsp cumin seeds

DIRECTIONS

1. Gently fry the spices in the ghee or oil for about 2-3 minutes. Add the rice and beans and cook for a further 2 minutes.
2. Cover with 6 cups of water, add the vegetable bouillon and bring to the boil. Stir briefly and lower the heat, cover and cook for 10-15 minutes until all the rice and lentils have soaked up the liquid.
3. Keep the pan covered and stir very occasionally. Ensure that the rice and beans are cooked and don't stick.
4. Add any vegetables at the end.

SPICED KICHADI WITH LEEK & SPRING ONION

INGREDIENTS:

- 1 tbsp bouillon
- ¼ cup of oil
- 1 cup of basmati rice
- 1 cup of red lentils or beans of choice (Some beans may need to be pre-soaked.)
- 3 cups of water
- spring onions
- small leek

Spices

- 1 tbsp coriander seeds
- 1 tbsp cardamom pod or less (tsp)
- 1 tbsp cumin seed
- 1 tbsp black peppercorn or less (tsp)
- 1 tbsp fennel
- 1 tsp whole clove or less (half)
- 1 cinnamon stick
- 1 pinch of saffron

DIRECTIONS

1. Heat the oil to very hot, tip in all the spices, and allow them to pop and infuse into the oil. Fry for about 2-3 minutes.
2. Add the onion or leeks and cook for a further 2-3 minutes. Be careful not to let the contents burn—keep stirring.
3. Add the rice and beans and cook for a further 2 minutes.
4. Cover with 3 cups of vegetable stock and bring to the boil. Stir briefly and lower the heat, cover and cook for approx. 10-15 minutes until all the rice and lentils have soaked up the liquid.
5. Keep the pan covered and stir occasionally. Ensure that the rice and beans are cooked and don't stick.

FENNEL KICHADI

This dish is an excellent purification food. It is a traditional Ayurvedic healing recipe that helps to feed, nourish and keep you satisfied.

INGREDIENTS

- 2 tbsp fennel seeds or fresh fennel bulb
- 1 cup of basmati rice
- ½ cup of red lentils
- 1½ cups of water
- ¼ tsp turmeric
- 1 tbsp cumin seeds
- 1 tsp sea salt
- 3 tbsp ghee/oil

DIRECTIONS

1. Boil the rice and skim off any foam. Whilst the rice is cooking
2. Put all other ingredients in a frying pan and fry lightly with the ghee/oil, then add to the rice and water and cook for about 20 minutes until the rice is cooked.
3. Add extra water if needed.
4. Serve with a side salad and cottage/vegan cheese.

KICHADI WITH PEAS

INGREDIENTS

- 1 cup of basmati rice
- ½ cup of yellow split mung/moong dhal
- 1 small bag of frozen peas
- 1 tbsp oil
- 4 cloves
- 1-inch stick of cinnamon
- 1 tsp mustard seeds
- 2 tsp grated ginger
- ½ tsp turmeric powder
- salt

DIRECTIONS

1. Wash the rice and moong dhal together and soak in hot water for an hour. Heat the oil in a saucepan and add the cloves, cinnamon and mustard seeds.
2. When the seeds crackle, add the ginger and sauté for 30 seconds.
3. Drain the oil from the spices and add the rice, moong dhal , turmeric powder and salt. Add 5 cups of water and mix well.
4. Add the frozen peas.
5. Bring to the boil, cover and simmer for 20-30 minutes.

KICHADI WITH SEASONAL VEGETABLES

INGREDIENTS

- 1 courgette, chopped
- 1 large tomato, chopped
- ½ tsp oil of your choice
- ½ cup of shredded coconut
- ½ tsp chilli powder or 1 fresh chilli (depending on how hot you like your food)

DIRECTIONS

Once you have cooked your *Basic Quick Foundation Kichadi on page 66*, melt the oil in a frying pan and fry the chopped courgettes, tomato, shredded coconut and chilli for a few minutes until slightly charred. Pile on top of your *Basic Quick Foundation Kichadi*.

TAHINI DRESSING WITH CUMIN & HONEY

This is a wonderful dressing to use on a range of dishes. Smooth, grounding tahini is a blend of sesame seeds often used in winter. Warm, pungent, and with the added tastes of cumin and delicious honey, tahini has been called the 'Liquid Sands of the Sahara'.

This delicious, versatile sauce can be used in a variety of ways:

- Pour over steamed or roasted vegetables
- Stir into a bowl of cooked rice
- Add to warm salads

INGREDIENTS

- 1 tsp cumin powder or freshly crushed cumin seeds
- 1 crushed clove of garlic (remove for Pitta)
- 1 tbsp runny honey - add honey at the end if heating the dressing.
- 5 finger pinch of Himalayan salt
- ¼ cup of tahini
- ¼ cup of water

DIRECTIONS

1. Blend all the ingredients, including the honey, in a blender if you want it cold (room temperature).
2. If you want it to be warm, which we love, blend all the ingredients, except for the honey, in the blender. Transfer them to a saucepan, gently stirring until it has warmed through. Take it off the heat and add the honey whilst it is warm but not hot.

VATA - OK
PITTA - in moderation
KAPHA - in moderation

TAHINI is heavy, oily, hot and sweet so can be aggravating for **Pitta** and **Kapha**.

PESTO WITH SPINACH AND OTHER LEAVES

The benefits of spinach are many. I really like using different leaves to make pesto. This one uses abundant spinach leaves. I personally love this spread on toasted sourdough bread and topped with avocado and cherry tomatoes. You need to be a bit careful as this recipe can be aggravating for Pitta, so it's only suggested now and then.

Low in fat and even lower in cholesterol, spinach is high in niacin and zinc, as well as protein, fibre, vitamins A, B6, C, E and K, thiamine, folate, calcium, iron, magnesium, phosphorus, potassium, copper and manganese. In other words, it's loaded with good things for every part of your body! To retain the rich iron content of spinach while cooking, lightly add lemon juice or white vinegar.

VATA - OK
PITTA - in moderation
KAPHA - OK

INGREDIENTS

- 400g pack of washed spinach leaves or use any dark leaves desired
- 2 garlic cloves, chopped
- 1 big handful of pine nuts or sliced almonds,
- 1 small handful of fresh basil, chopped
- 3 tsp olive oil
- Himalayan salt

DIRECTIONS

1. Dry roast your nuts in a frying pan for a couple of minutes.
2. Place a few spinach leaves, garlic, dry roasted pine nuts, basil and a little oil in a blender and blend until leaves begin to disintegrate. Keep adding spinach leaves a few at a time with small amounts of oil to the blender and use a wooden spoon to keep combining the mixture. Process until the spinach pesto mixture is smooth. Add salt to taste.
3. You can also use this pesto for a pasta dish.

ASPARAGUS & NUT CRUNCHY PÂTÉ

We need to take advantage of the glut of fresh greens that arrive in the markets, asparagus being one of them. Out-of-season or force-grown asparagus makes them tough and stringy. Buy them young and fresh for the best benefits. This is an unusual but fresh pâté to have for breakfast or a light lunch full of goodness.

The recipe includes cheese. Ayurveda doesn't really favour cheese, but it's the hard cheese that creates digestive problems, so only eat now and then to take care of your digestive health.

Choose your favourite nuts, remembering your dosha and what suits you most.

VATA – most nuts

PITTA – almonds are best

KAPHA – almonds are best

INGREDIENTS

- 1 handful of chopped/crushed nuts
- 1 bunch of asparagus
- 1 small tub of cream cheese.
- 2 tbsps crème fraiche
- 2 tbsps chives, chopped
- 1 tbsp fresh mint leaves
- 1 tbsp lemon juice

DIRECTIONS

1. Rinse and prepare the asparagus by removing the woody ends. Cook by steaming or dry frying for up to 8 minutes, keeping it crunchy but cooked.
2. In the meantime, mix the remaining ingredients in a bowl, folding in the nuts, chives and leaves.
3. Chop the cooked asparagus into small chunks and add to the mixture.
4. Serve piled on top of flatbread or toast.

ASPARAGUS is good for all types. You can add other varieties of nuts for a change but stay with mainly almonds for **Pitta** and **Kapha**.

SPICED CARROT SALAD

This Spiced Carrot Salad is a family favourite with its combination of fresh carrots tossed with aromatic spices and herbs, creating a harmonious blend of delicious textures. The crispness of the carrots contrasts with the spices, while the herbs add freshness. This vibrant salad offers a refreshing and nutritious option, perfect for a light lunch or a side dish to complement any meal.

VATA – OK
PITTA – reduce garlic
KAPHA – reduce fruit, if adding

INGREDIENTS

- 500g carrots, thinly cut diagonally into long strips
- ¼ cup extra-virgin olive oil or coconut oil
- 3 tbsp fresh lemon juice
- ½ cup of chopped fresh coriander and/or parsley
- 2 cloves garlic, mashed
- ½ tsp ground cumin
- ½ tsp ground cinnamon
- 1 tsp sweet paprika
- 1 pinch of salt
- 1 tsp minced green chillies or ¼ tsp cayenne (optional)
- selection of dried fruit like currants, raisins or cranberries to add extra texture and taste
- yoghurt to serve

DIRECTIONS

Cook the carrot strips in water for about 10 minutes to soften them but keep them firm. Drain and toss the carrots and fruit, if using, then add all the remaining ingredients and leave to marinate, the longer you leave this dish, the better the taste. We recommend at least a couple of hours, or if you prepare it earlier, you can leave it overnight. Serve it with a spoonful of yoghurt.

SWEETS

Ayurveda loves sweets and puddings. They are considered an important part of a balanced diet when consumed in moderation and prepared using wholesome ingredients.

Ayurveda emphasises the use of natural sweeteners like jaggery, honey, maple syrup and dates instead of refined sugars. These offer sweetness as well as nutritional benefits.

Incorporating digestive spices like cardamom, cinnamon, ginger and nutmeg into sweets and puddings helps improve digestion and enhances flavour. These spices also add warmth and aroma to the dishes.

Using seasonal and locally available ingredients such as fruits, nuts and grains in sweets and puddings, ensures that they are fresh, nutritious and aligned with nature's rhythms.

Pay attention to portion sizes and avoid overindulging to maintain balance and prevent imbalances in the body.

SCRUMPTIOUS SQUASH CAKE

This is a really scrumptious cake but should be eaten fairly quickly and warm, if possible, it is really filling and really good for a hearty snack or afternoon treat.

INGREDIENTS

- 3 cups of all-purpose flour
- 1 cup of coconut sugar
- 1 tsp baking soda
- ½ tsp baking powder
- 1 tsp ground cinnamon
- ½ tsp salt
- ½ tsp ground nutmeg
- ¼ tsp ground cloves
- 2 large eggs
- 1 cup of cooked butternut squash, mashed/pureed)
- ½ cup of olive or canola oil
- ½ cup of water
- ½ cup of chopped walnuts and almonds
- blueberries that have been lightly cooked so they are oozing are great with these scones and/or cream of your choice

DIRECTIONS

1. Preheat the oven to Gas 4/350°F/180°C.
2. Whisk all the wet ingredients in a bowl or jug. Mix the dry ingredients with the wet ingredients; the mixture should be nice and sticky.
3. Make sure you grease the tin well.
4. Cook for about 35-45 minutes and check with a skewer that it's cooked inside. Your skewer should come out clean once cooked. Cool a little before you remove it from the tin. Slice and drizzle with the icing. Serve with blueberries and cream. Yummy!

Icing sugar drizzle *(optional)*

5. Mix regular icing sugar with coconut icing sugar. You can make coconut icing sugar by blitzing coconut sugar and turning it into the finer sugar needed for icing. It doesn't have to be perfect because you are only drizzling on top
6. Mix half and half sugars and add water until it is shiny, think just pouring consistency and then drizzle across your cake.

VATA – OK
PITTA – OK
KAPHA – Most breads, scones etc. are not suitable for Kapha as they are heavy and dry. Kapha should eat only in moderation and small quantities.

HYDRATING SUPER FRUIT IN A BOWL

In Ayurveda, hydrating fruits are valued for their ability to replenish fluids, cool the body and support overall health and well-being, especially during hot seasons or for individuals with Pitta dosha predominance.

INGREDIENTS

- 2 cucumbers
- 2 apples
- ¼ cooked beetroot
- 1 handful of strawberries pomegranate seeds blueberries
- ½ banana very thinly sliced half of a banana (you can use any fruit you like)
- 1 handful of sunflower seeds.
- 1 tbsp flaxseed oil
- 1 tub of non-fat organic yoghurt or plant-based yoghurt

DIRECTIONS

1. Peel the cucumber and apples close to the body of the fruit. Blend or chop your remaining fruit until it's very small and mix it together with the cucumber and apples.
2. Mix in the flaxseed oil.
3. Place in a beautiful bowl, sprinkle on the seeds and toss your fruit into the yoghurt.
4. Eat slowly. Eating fruit slowly allows you to savour its flavours and aids in better digestion and nutrient absorption.

PARSNIP CAKE

This recipe has been adapted from one my mother gave me from an old cookery book. If you like carrot cake, you will love this parsnip version. It's moist, full of goodness, and it's delicious.

INGREDIENTS

- 4 large eggs
- 2 cups of sugar (We use soft brown sugar.)
- 1 ½ cups coconut oil
- 2 cups all-purpose flour
- 2 tsp baking powder
- 1/2 tsp salt
- 2 tsp ground cinnamon
- 2 tbsp grated fresh ginger

DIRECTIONS

1. Preheat your oven to Gas 4/350°F/180°C
2. Butter or line a 12-inch cake tin.
3. Beat the eggs into the sugar, add the eggs one at a time, combining thoroughly before adding the next egg. Beat the oil into the mixture, then add the flour, baking powder, salt, cinnamon, ginger, ½ tsp mustard powder, ½ tsp grated nutmeg, cup of chopped pecan nuts, ½ cup of currants, 2 cups of grated peeled parsnips, mustard powder and nutmeg until completely combined.
4. Fold in the nuts, currants and grated parsnips.
5. Pour into your prepared cake tin and bake for about 1 hour and 20 minutes in the centre of the oven.
6. Leave it to cool before covering it with the frosting, or you can leave it plain.

CREAM CHEESE FROSTING

I'm using a traditional cream cheese and sugar frosting, but you can substitute with sugar-free frosting and vegan frostings.

INGREDIENTS

- 1 cup of cream cheese
- ¼ cup of unsalted butter – warmed to room temperature
- 1 cup of confectioners icing sugar
- 2 tsp vanilla extract
- pecans, lemon or orange peel to decorate

DIRECTIONS

1. Place all the ingredients into a mixer or use a hand beater until the frosting is smooth.
2. Cover the top of your cake and decorate with pecan nuts or grated peel. Delicious!

RAW HEALTHY CHOC OAT FUDGE SNACK

This guilt-free but indulgent sweet combines ingredients like raw cacao powder, dates, chickpeas and oats. It's satisfyingly sweet without the need for baking, and it can be enjoyed as bite-sized balls or pressed into bars.

INGREDIENTS

- 1 cup of oats
- 1 cup of chickpeas or 400g can
- ¾ cup of cashew butter
- ¼ cup of maple or rice malt syrup
- 1 tsp vanilla paste
- ½ tsp Himalayan salt
- 1 cup of plant-based milk or water
- 1 cup of roughly chopped dark chocolate

Chocolate topping *(optional)*

- 1 cup of roughly chopped cacao butter
- ½ cup of raw cacao powder or dark cocoa powder
- ¼ cup of coconut cream
- ¼ cup of rice malt or maple syrup

DIRECTIONS

1. Blitz the oats in a blender until like breadcrumbs. Add more oats for a chunkier texture.
2. Add the chickpeas, cashew butter, syrup, vanilla and salt until it forms a thick paste. Add more liquid until it's like a fudge texture.
3. Add the chopped chocolate. Scoop out the mixture and press into a shallow cake/brownie tin. Put in the fridge while you make the topping.

Chocolate topping *(optional)*

4. Melt all the ingredients gently in a small saucepan and mix thoroughly. Whisk with a hand whisk as it gets cooler and thicker. When smooth, pour onto the yummy chocolate brownie mixture. Place into the fridge again for a few hours or overnight.
5. Cut with a hot knife by heating a knife blade in very hot water.

POMEGRANATE, ROASTED ALMONDS & GRILLED PEACHES

This is a wonderful medley combination of pomegranate, roasted almonds and juicy peaches. The tart sweetness of pomegranate seeds pairs perfectly with the nutty crunch of roasted almonds, while the succulent ripe peaches make it a real treat. This trio is a harmonious blend of textures and tastes.

This is a simply gorgeous dish and not one that you would expect to eat for Kapha, but it's a treat.

If you are willing to understand the flavours and the way that you can change the constitution of food sources, we can use some foods that we would otherwise eat in minor ways. This is quite a sweet dish. Eat it in small portions.

So enjoy this and keep your plate portions smallish.

INGREDIENTS

- 1 pomegranate – ½ for Vata
- 2 peaches – cook for Kapha and Pitta
- 1 handful of almonds
- lemon juice
- 1 tsp coconut sugar (This is not sugar. It's made from the flower of the coconut plant and has a caramel flavour.)
- mint leaves, chopped *(optional)*

DIRECTIONS

1. Preheat your grill.
2. Remove the seeds from the pomegranate.
3. Peel and slice the peaches. If you want to be super Kapha-conscious, you can use apple slices. Roast the almonds in a dry pan until they become a little golden. Add the coconut sugar and gently fry. Then, add the lemon juice and stir it all together.
4. In the meantime, put your slices of fruit on some tin foil and place them under a hot grill for a few minutes until they just start to catch at the edges.
5. Plate the fruit, spoon over the almonds and add the pomegranate seeds. Eat immediately. Sprinkle the mint on top.

RHUBARB & CHERRY CRUMBLE

RHUBARB is sweet, sour and bitter and is fine for all doshas.

KAPHA should use less sugar and eat in moderation and smaller portions.

CHERRIES contain lots of fibre so help digestion. They are good for **Vata** and **Kapha**. **Pitta** can eat this crumble with the other ingredients, but cherries alone will aggravate **Pitta**.

This recipe holds a special place in my heart, as it's based on a favourite dish that my mother used to make for me when I was a child. Every time my mother prepared it, the aroma would fill our home, and I knew a delicious treat was in store. Recreating this recipe brings back cherished memories of family gatherings and shared meals around the table. It's not just about the flavours and ingredients; it's about the love and care that went into each dish, making it taste all the more special.

INGREDIENTS

- 1 bunch of rhubarb, cut into small chunks or tinned rhubarb
- 1 small tin/jar of cherries in syrup – this gives it the sweetness.
- 3 tbsp coconut sugar – less if you don't want it to be too sweet

Crumble

- 1½ cups of all-purpose flour
- ¾ cup of light-brown sugar or coconut sugar
- 100g ghee or plain butter, cubed

DIRECTIONS

1. Preheat oven to Gas 4/350°F/180°C.
2. Put the rhubarb and sugar in a pan and gently heat until the rhubarb starts to soften. It's important to mix in the cherries at this stage. If you use fresh cherries, they will take a little longer before going soft. Don't completely cook through, as it will continue to cook in the oven with the crumble.
3. In a separate bowl, add the butter cubes to the flour and work with your fingers to make a crumbly mixture until it looks like breadcrumbs. Pour the rhubarb mixture into an ovenproof dish and sprinkle the crumble over the top. Cook for 35-40 minutes until the top is golden brown and the rhubarb is bubbling at the edges. Serve this with homemade custard—it just has to be!

APPLE, PLUM & DATE CRUMBLE

This recipe offers a great alternative to the Rhubarb & Cherry Crumble, drawing inspiration from my mother's recipes. This one brings a fresh twist to the table. It's a testament to the versatility and creativity in the Ayurveda Kitchen, where we can explore new flavours and ingredients while honouring cherished traditions.

INGREDIENTS

- 500g apples and plums or pears – make sure you use green apples with a bit of tartness.
- 1 tsp cinnamon
- 6 big dates - a couple more if you want it sweeter
- 1 cup of almond flour
- ½ cup of gluten-free oats or muesli
- ½ cup of soft vegan butter
- 4 tbsp almond flakes

DIRECTIONS

1. Preheat oven to Gas 4/350°F/180°C. Chop up your fruit, dates, etc., add them to a pan with cinnamon and gently stew for 15 minutes.
2. Pour into an ovenproof or smaller individual dishes.
3. In a separate bowl, make your crumble by rubbing the butter into the almond flour and oats until you have a crumbly texture. Sprinkle the crumble over your fruit and finish with almond flakes. Cook for about 25 minutes until golden. Enjoy with non-dairy cream.

CLEANSING STEWED APPLES AND PEARS

The cleansing and nourishing properties of stewed apples and pears offer a simple, soothing recipe rooted in Ayurveda principles. Cooked with warming spices like cinnamon, ginger and cloves, this comforting concoction helps balance the body's energies and promote digestive health. In Ayurveda, stewed fruits are believed to aid in detoxification while providing essential nutrients to the body.

INGREDIENTS

- 1 apple – *organic if possible*
- 1 pear – *organic if possible*
- 12 raisins
- 1 clove
- 1 pinch of powdered cinnamon water
- squeeze of lemon juice

DIRECTIONS

1. Peel as close to the fruit as possible, then cut it into small chunks. Add the fruit to a saucepan, cover it with water, and add the raisins, cloves and cinnamon.
2. Cook for about 20 minutes until the fruit is soft.
3. Squeeze a teaspoon of lemon juice over the stewed fruit and eat whilst it is still warm.

TIP – If you cook the fruit longer until it is very mushy, it will make a simple chutney once it is cooled.

DIVINE ROSE LATTE PUDDING

This is an extravagant but simple recipe that is worth having as a divine drink or pudding anytime. It uses organic dried rose petals, which you can quite easily get online nowadays. According to Ayurveda, rose is considered a loving and compassionate flower and we all know it's favoured by romantics and symbolises love. The taste is fragrant and divine, bringing some necessary serenity to your day. Mixed with nuts or seeds, it can also give a good protein hit.

INGREDIENTS

Rosa Jam

- 1 cup of mineral water
- 1 cup of organic rose petals
- 5 tbsp rice syrup

Latte

- 1 cup of soaked nuts (Soak for a few hours or overnight. This helps to liquidise them more easily, making them extra digestible. You can use cashew nuts, almonds, sunflower seeds, pine nuts, etc.)
- 1 mug of water
- 1 mug of milk of your choice
- 2 tsp vanilla essence
- 2 tsp rosa jam

DIRECTIONS

Rosa Jam

1. Put the ingredients into a heavy saucepan and bring to the boil. Reduce heat immediately and simmer for about 15 minutes until it's jam-like. If you need to add a little extra water, that's fine. Once it's cooked, let it cool a little, then transfer to a glass jar.

Latte

2. Simply blitz all your ingredients. You can have this warm or cold. Then, just sit for a while as you experience the wonderful fragrant rose latte.
3. We love to add a teaspoon of caffeine-free coffee for an alternative and delicious coffee latte.

YUMMY CHOCOLATE CHIA LATTE GLASS

So very decadent and yet so healthy. This is full of great benefits and is quick and simple to make. Chia seeds have many benefits, far too many to mention in this recipe.

They are an excellent source of omega-3 fatty acids, rich in antioxidants, and they provide fibre, iron, and calcium. Omega-3 fatty acids help raise HDL cholesterol—the good cholesterol that protects against heart attacks and strokes.

VATA - in moderation
PITTA - in moderation
KAPHA - use ordinary water, low fat yoghurt, 1 tsp maple syrup, 1 tbsp coconut oil

INGREDIENTS

- 1 cup of chia seeds
- 3 cups of coconut water
- 2 tbsp coconut oil
- 2 tbsp cacao powder
- 2 tbsp coconut yoghurt
- 1 tbsp maple syrup
- selection of mixed berries of your choice
- selection of your favourite chopped nuts and seeds

DIRECTIONS

1. Combine the chia seeds in the coconut water and leave the mixture to thicken for about an hour. Stir occasionally.
2. When the chia seeds are ready, heat the coconut oil in a saucepan and add the chia mixture, cacao powder and maple syrup, stirring well. Take your pan off the heat and layer in glasses with your berries and yoghurt. Top with the coconut yoghurt and finish with a sprinkle of nuts and seeds.

CHIA SEEDS soak up moisture in the body so are great for Kapha. This is less so for Pitta and even lesser for Vata.

ORANGE COUSCOUS PUDDING

This is a delightful harmony of pairing of orange and couscous. The vibrant, citrusy notes of orange complement the subtle nuttiness of couscous, creating a refreshing and satisfying combination. When it's tossed together with added raisins, it's a delicious, sweet salad.

INGREDIENTS

- Couscous – follow packet instructions (Cook enough couscous for 2-3 people depending on how hungry you are.)
- 1 large organic orange, grate the zest and squeeze out the juice
- 1 handful of golden raisins - soaked for 30 minutes in hot water 1 handful of cashew nuts - soaked for 30 minutes in hot water
- ½ tsp ground cinnamon
- plain yoghurt for serving

DIRECTIONS

Once your couscous is made, add all the other ingredients and toss together. You can throw a handful of fruit on top, but if you do, only serve it with plant-based yoghurt. Ayurveda warns us against eating dairy and fruit together as it is difficult for digestion, which is why we suggest cooking the fruit first. Serve in bowls and top with yoghurt. This makes a great breakfast as well.

CREAMY RICE WITH STEM GINGER

A comforting combination of creamy rice and zesty ginger. The velvety texture of the rice is beautifully enhanced by the warm, aromatic flavour of ginger, creating a harmonious balance of richness and spice that will warm your soul. From a jar of stem ginger in syrup, extract your first two ingredients.

INGREDIENTS

- 1 tbsp stem ginger syrup
- 2 pieces of stem ginger, chopped into small pieces
- 2 pieces of fresh ginger, chopped small
- 2 tbsp sugar (We use coconut sugar.)
- 1 cup of short-grain rice (We use basmati.)
- 1 tsp vanilla bean paste
- 2 cups of milk
- ½ small tub of cream

DIRECTIONS

1. Add the sugar, stem ginger, syrup, milk and vanilla into a saucepan and heat until simmering.
2. Add the rice and stir so it doesn't stick. Once the rice is tender, remove it from the heat and let it cool a little, then fold in as much cream as you fancy—we add about 2 tablespoons.
3. Drizzle with some ginger syrup and sprinkle ginger pieces on top.

DRINKS

In Ayurveda, beverages are considered an essential part of maintaining balance and promoting health. We have included a variety of traditional drinks for exploring throughout the day.

Ayurveda reminds us never to drink iced beverages as it will delete the Agni, the fire in the belly, which is the digestive system.

Drinking warm water, especially first thing in the morning or throughout the day, is believed to help stimulate digestion, cleanse toxins from the body and promote hydration. It's a simple yet effective way to support overall well-being.

At the very least, drink at room temperature. Herbal teas made from Ayurvedic herbs and spices such as ginger, turmeric, cinnamon, cardamom and liquorice are commonly used for their therapeutic properties.

These teas can help improve digestion, boost immunity, reduce inflammation and promote relaxation.

Turmeric and Ginger are considered valuable in Ayurveda.

TURMERIC

The anti-inflammatory properties of turmeric are great for the overheated body that can suffer from heat-related pain.

Turmeric is used in Ayurveda to balance Vata, Pitta, and Kapha, although, in excess, it can aggravate Pitta and Vata.

It has a particularly beneficial effect for Rasa and Rakta Dhatus (the blood and plasma of the circulatory system). It also kindles Agni (digestive fire), helping reduce Kapha and Ama (toxins).

GINGER

Ayurveda calls ginger the 'universal medicine'. It has been used for centuries and is still one of the most popular herbs of Ayurveda.

If you search the internet, you will see there are masses of information and trials being conducted using ginger.

According to Ayurveda, ginger is considered a potent medicinal herb due to its ability to enhance digestion, boost immunity and alleviate various ailments such as nausea and inflammation. Its warming properties are believed to balance the body's energies and promote overall well-being.

TURMERIC LATTE

Turmeric Latte — often called golden milk — is a warm beverage made with milk (dairy or plant-based) and turmeric, along with other spices like ginger, cinnamon and black pepper. It's known for its anti-inflammatory and immune-boosting properties and is often consumed before bedtime to promote relaxation and improve sleep quality.

VATA - OK
PITTA - Coconut milk is more acceptable
KAPHA - OK

INGREDIENTS

- 2 cups of coconut, oat or almond milk (can be made at home from dried ingredients)
- 1 tbsp organic flaxseed or coconut oil
- 1 tsp ground turmeric
- 2/3 cardamom pods
- 1 cinnamon stick or 1 tsp ground cinnamon
- 1 tbsp honey or agave

DIRECTIONS

1. Put all the ingredients (except the honey/agave) into a saucepan, whisk and bring carefully to the boil. Reduce the heat to low and simmer for 15 minutes.
2. Strain the milk through a sieve or muslin if you wish.
3. Add honey/agave and a sprinkle of cinnamon, and drink while it's warm.

The anti-inflammatory properties of **TURMERIC** are great for the overheated body that can suffer from heat-related pain.

ENERGISING TURMERIC MORNING JUICE

The anti-inflammatory properties of turmeric are great for the overheated body that can suffer from heat-related pain.

Turmeric is used in Ayurveda to balance Vata, Pitta and Kapha, though, in excess, it can aggravate Pitta and Vata.

It has a particularly beneficial effect for Rasa and Rakta Dhatus (the blood and plasma of the circulatory system). It also kindles Agni (digestive fire), helping reduce Kapha and Ama (toxins).

VATA - OK
PITTA - in moderation
KAPHA - OK

INGREDIENTS

- 1-inch piece of turmeric root or 1-2 tsp ground turmeric powder
- 1 whole cucumber
- 1 stalk of celery
- ½ thumb size piece of ginger
- 1 peeled lemon - use lime for Pitta

DIRECTIONS

Juice all ingredients and drink immediately.

TURMERIC TEA – WITH A DIFFERENCE

VATA – OK
PITTA – in moderation
KAPHA – OK

A simple, easy drink that can be sipped throughout the day.

Turmeric has a host of benefits but is mostly known for its anti-inflammatory properties. Turmeric is light, hot and dry and can aggravate the Pitta dosha if Pitta is high as it stimulates Pitta qualities.

INGREDIENTS

- ½ stick of cinnamon or ½ tsp ground
- 1 clove
- 1 pinch of nutmeg
- 1 pinch of black pepper
- 1 tsp grated fresh ginger
- 1 tsp turmeric
- squeeze of lemon
- 2 cups of water
- honey or agave

DIRECTIONS

Put everything into a small saucepan, bring to the boil and then simmer for 5 minutes. Strain through a sieve and taste. You can add more water if it's too strong. Sip throughout the day.

GINGER TEA

This is a favourite of ours; it's an all-rounder for sure. Drink it twice a day for a good detoxing effect or once a day to bring your system into action. For a traditional cold and flu tea, add honey and lemon.

INGREDIENTS

- fresh ginger – we recommend using a one-inch piece of ginger per cup of tea
- fresh lemon – *optional*
- honey – *optional*

DIRECTIONS

1. Thinly slice your fresh ginger. You don't need to peel it first; just rinse and scrub off any visible dirt.
2. In a saucepan, combine the ginger with fresh water (use one cup of water per serving). Bring the mixture to the boil over a high heat. Reduce the heat to a gentle simmer for 5 minutes (10 minutes if you want extra-strong tea).
3. Pour the tea through a fine sieve to catch all the ginger. If desired, serve your tea with a thin round of lemon or honey.

PEPPERMINT TEA

Peppermint Tea—the benefits are many. It aids digestion, relieves stomach problems, eases irritable bowel symptoms, lessens constipation, settles nausea, reduces fever and coughs, boosts immune systems, sweetens bad breath and relieves stress.

INGREDIENTS

- mint leaves or dried mint
- honey
- lemon juice

DIRECTIONS

1. Boil 2 cups of water and add 15 to 20 fresh mint leaves. Alternatively, 1 tsp dried mint can be used. Turn off the heat and allow your liquid to steep for 10-15 minutes or until your desired strength is achieved.
2. Strain through a sieve or muslin cloth (or chew them if you don't mind the texture and they are small) and serve warm with a drizzle of honey and a squeeze of lemon.

HERBAL AYURVEDA CCF TEA

CCF tea, also known as cumin, coriander and fennel tea, is a popular Ayurvedic herbal infusion known for its digestive benefits and soothing properties. This ancient blend combines the earthy warmth of cumin, the citrusy notes of coriander, and the sweet, liquorice-like flavour of fennel. CCF tea promotes healthy digestion, alleviates bloating and reduces gas and discomfort after meals. It's often enjoyed throughout the day, particularly after meals, to support optimal digestion and overall well-being.

A traditional ancient tea for all body types. Make your own for a greater and more effective cleanse.

VATA - OK
PITTA - OK
KAPHA - OK

INGREDIENTS

- 1 pint of boiled water
- ½ tsp cumin seeds
- ½ tsp coriander seeds
- ½ tsp fennel seeds

DIRECTIONS

1. Boil the water, add the spices, then let it steep for 10 minutes with the lid on.
2. Strain out the spices through a sieve, pour the water into a thermal flask and sip throughout the day. Make a new batch of tea each day.

CCF (CUMIN, CORIANDER AND FENNEL) TEA is an all-round tridoshic herbal drink to help balance and cleanse all doshas.

TURMERIC MORNING ZING SHOT

A Turmeric Morning Zing Shot is a vibrant and invigorating concoction designed to jumpstart your day with a burst of energy and vitality.

VATA - OK
PITTA - in moderation
KAPHA - OK

INGREDIENTS

- 2 small oranges, peeled 1 small lemon, peeled
- 1 small lime, peeled
- 1-inch piece of ginger, cut into slices
- 2 tsp ground turmeric – *read Turmeric panel below*
- pinch black pepper
- 1 tbsp honey or agave 1 pinch of sea salt
- ⅓ cup of water
- 2 stems of fresh coriander
- 1 chunk of pineapple – pineapple will aggravate Pitta

DIRECTIONS

1. Grate or juice the turmeric and pineapple. If juicing, you can add the fresh coriander; otherwise, chop it finely. You can pound the grated ingredients in a mortar and pestle and add the pepper.
2. Whisk in a little water and drink in a shot!

FRESH TURMERIC is the best to use, and you can grate using a ginger grater. If not, use a turmeric tablet or a quarter of a teaspoon of ground turmeric. The ground form will be powdery, which is why fresh is better. Have a go at grating fresh, but remember to wear gloves as your hands will stain yellow. Adding a pinch of black pepper activates the turmeric and sends it into the system much quicker.

SUPER BREAKFAST FRUIT & SPICE SHOTS

Are you looking for a kick-start to the day? Then, these easy and super simple morning shots will do the trick. These are full of energising properties and have lots of other benefits. If you need something quick before you move into your morning routine, try one of these. You will find your favourite among them, and you can adapt the recipe to suit what you need.

Always follow your shots with a glass of water to help the energising properties flood through you as quickly as possible. Remember that these are short-term hits for energy, not unlike your coffee hit, but much better for you.

You need to be a bit inventive in making these shots so that you don't have to spend much time preparing them. Here are some ideas.

LIME MORNING HOT SHOT

VATA - OK
PITTA - OK
KAPHA - OK

- juice of half a lime
- ½ tsp organic runny honey
- 1 pinch of cayenne pepper
- 2 stems of fresh coriander

DIRECTIONS

Chop the coriander into tiny pieces and crush it in a mortar and pestle. Add the lime juice and pepper and whisk with a little extra water. Drink immediately.

GINGER ELIXIR MORNING SHOT

VATA - OK
PITTA - in moderation
KAPHA - OK

- 1 tsp grated fresh ginger
- juice of half a small lemon
- ½ tsp organic runny honey
- 1 pinch of black pepper

DIRECTIONS

Mash the grated ginger in a mortar and pestle. Add the lemon, honey and pepper and whisk with a little extra water. Drink straight away.

GREEN JUICE

Green Juice made from cucumber, celery, spinach, kale, apple and mint is rejuvenating. It aligns perfectly with Ayurvedic principles of balance and holistic health and the ability to support detoxification, digestion and vitality. With its high-water content and cooling nature, cucumber is considered tridoshic in Ayurveda, meaning it balances all three doshas, Vata, Pitta and Kapha. It helps pacify excess heat in the body, soothes inflammation and aids in gentle detoxification by flushing out toxins. Celery is valued in Ayurveda for its ability to stimulate Agni, the digestive fire, without aggravating Pitta. It supports the elimination of Ama (toxins) from the body and promotes healthy digestion and assimilation of nutrients.

Leafy greens like spinach and kale are chosen for their abundant nutrients and Prana (life force energy). They are considered sattvic foods, promoting clarity, vitality and spiritual growth.

Spinach and kale nourish the body at a deep level, supporting overall health and well-being.

In Ayurveda, sweet fruits like apples are considered nourishing and balancing for all doshas when consumed in moderation. Apples provide natural sweetness to the juice while offering fibre and antioxidants to support digestion and detoxification. Add mint for its cooling and digestive properties. It helps alleviate Pitta imbalances, soothes the stomach, and enhances Agni, making it easier to digest food and eliminate waste.

Regularly drinking this Ayurvedic Green Juice can help restore balance to the doshas, promote Agni and support optimal health and vitality.

INGREDIENTS

- ½ cucumber
- 3 sticks of celery
- 1 handful of spinach 1 handful of kale
- 1 green apple
- 1 small handful of mint

DIRECTIONS

And... juice!

MASALAS

Ayurveda masalas are traditional spice blends that hold immense significance in Ayurvedic cooking and holistic health practices. These mixtures consist of various herbs, spices and botanicals, each selected for its unique flavour profile and therapeutic properties.

In Ayurveda, masalas are not only used to enhance the taste of dishes but also to promote balance and well-being within the body and mind. Each spice within the masala blend carries specific qualities that can influence the doshas (Vata, Pitta and Kapha), the fundamental energies that govern our physical and mental constitution according to Ayurvedic principles.

Ayurvedic masalas support overall digestion, boost immunity and aid in detoxification. They are also thought to have anti-inflammatory, antioxidant and antimicrobial properties, making them valuable additions to a holistic wellness routine.

MAKE YOUR OWN GARAM MASALA/SPICE MIX

There are lots of different recipes for garam masalas, and this is just one of them.

The fresher the spice mix, the more fragrant it will be. Don't make too much and store the remainder in a screw-top jar. The masala will last for about a month; it won't go off, but it will lose some of its flavour and fragrance.

Add the required amount to your food. We tend to use half to a teaspoon in most recipes, but it's best to taste it to suit your own requirements.

VATA – OK
PITTA – heating so in moderation
KAPHA – OK

INGREDIENTS

- 2 tbsp coriander seeds
- 1 tbsp cumin seeds
- 1 tbsp cardamom seeds
- 1 tbsp whole black peppercorns
- 1 tsp fennel seeds
- 1 tsp mustard seeds
- ½ tsp whole cloves
- 1 dried red chilli pepper, seeds removed
- 2 tbsp ground turmeric

DIRECTIONS

1. Combine the coriander, cumin, cardamom, peppercorns, fennel, mustard, cloves and red chilli pepper in a small frying pan. Toast gently for 2 minutes until fragrant. Be careful not to burn the spices.
2. Grind the toasted spices in a mortar and pestle or spice grinder. We don't mind having tiny bits of the spices in our mix, so we always use a mortar and pestle. Add the turmeric to the mix and transfer everything to a jar. Always give your jar a good shake, as this combines the spices before adding them to recipes.

VATA MASALA SPICE MIX

VATA AGGRAVATED

When Vata dosha is aggravated, you will feel out of balance, and you will feel this in a variety of ways, from dry skin, aching bones, feeling the cold much more, and being more worried, nervous and erratic. Your digestive system will also suffer as the body and digestion are weakened by the excess cold felt by Vata. Indigestion for Vata results in wind, tummy tension and pain due to the body feeling stiffer and rigid, which is caused by the colder, dryer nature of Vata.

To help bring Vata into balance, warming herbs and spices that stimulate and regulate digestion while soothing the nerves and muscles are used.

BENEFITS OF USING A VATA MASALA SPICE MIX

It helps to bring balance to the dosha and aids with digestive problems caused by many factors such as alcohol, medicines, reflux, infections, stress, etc. Vata symptoms include bloating, feeling sick, indigestion and burning stomach.

It also helps to reduce constipation caused by aggravated Vata, which is dry and cold. Constipation leads to the accumulation of toxins, which affect overall health and well-being. Ayurveda sees constipation as a reason for many other conditions like dandruff, acne, boils, skin disorders, hair loss, etc. When you are constipated, toxins or waste remain in the intestines and get absorbed into the bloodstream, lowering immunity and promoting ill health.

SIMPLE LIFESTYLE CHANGES

Meditation, yoga and pranayama can reduce worry and anxiety. Warm, oily foods will help balance the cold qualities in Vata. Wrap up warm in cold seasons and increase fluids. Opt for low-fat dairy, soft foods, cooked vegetables and sweet and heavy fruits. Avoid raw vegetables and cold foods. Minimise spicy, dry, crunchy, astringent and bitter foods while favouring warm, sour, sweet and oily foods.

The word 'masala' simply means a combination of ground spices.

According to Ayurveda, **Vata** is the body type/dosha that is formed from the combination of the air and ether elements, with the qualities of being dry, light, cold, rough, subtle and mobile.

INGREDIENTS

- 3 tsp ground fennel seeds *(Foundation Spice)*
- 1 tsp ground turmeric
- 1 tsp ground cumin
- ½ tsp ground ginger
- ¼-½ tsp black pepper
- 1 tsp ground cardamom
- 1 tsp Himalayan salt
- 1 tsp ground cinnamon
- ½ tsp ground cloves

DIRECTIONS

1. Your spice mix will always taste better if you grind each spice yourself. For all ground spices, mix well and store them in an airtight container.
2. Add spices to hot water for a spiced tea, or lightly cook into ghee or your favourite cooking oil to drizzle on vegetables.
3. Sprinkle on foods while cooking or add to finished meals like soups, salads, sandwiches, stews, rice, casseroles, pasta dishes, vegetables, etc.

PITTA MASALA SPICE MIX

AGGRAVATED PITTA

Excess Pitta causes increased heat, sharpness and oiliness in the digestive tract. It inflames the digestive fire, creating acidic conditions that can lead to conditions like indigestion and acidity.

PITTA dosha is a combination of the elements fire and water. It controls digestion, metabolism and energy production. It has the quality of being hot, sharp, liquid and oily.

BENEFITS OF USING A PITTA MASALA SPICE MIX

It improves digestion by neutralising stomach acids and removing excess heat from the system. It is cooling, calming, cleansing and nurturing, and it helps with the symptoms of indigestion, including feelings of fullness, gas, belching, nausea, and burning in the stomach while regulating the metabolism. Pitta imbalance almost always begins with a problem in the internal digestive fire, which manifests in various forms of hyperacidity, inflammation, and indigestion. It helps reduce acid reflux and other medical problems like heartburn, throat irritation, hoarseness, asthma, chest pain, dental erosion, regurgitation, etc. Aggravated Pitta can manifest in the form of skin inflammations, rashes, digestive trouble, impatience, anger, short temper, skipping meals and poor sleep.

SIMPLE LIFESTYLE CHANGES

Stay cool, particularly in warmer seasons, and avoid vigorous activity or exercise.

Do not over drink, particularly whilst eating. This can disrupt the digestive fire of Pitta. Yoga, meditation and laughing therapy reduce anger and aggravation. Meditation, in the form of gratitude, is useful, as well as swimming and staying out of the sun. Make sure you choose natural, cool fabrics for clothing and favour cool or warm foods rather than hot and spicy. Pitta foods include bitter, sweet and astringent tastes and include sweet and cooling fruits. Bitter foods include green tea, green leaves, broccoli, asparagus, turmeric, etc. Avoid or reduce sour and pungent foods and drink coconut water. Cooling showers before bedtime help to cool the body.

INGREDIENTS

- 6 tsp ground fennel seeds *(Foundation Spice)*
- 2 tsp ground coriander
- 2 tsp ground cumin
- 1 tsp turmeric
- 1 tsp cardamom
- 1 tsp ginger

DIRECTIONS

1. Your spice mix will always taste better if you grind each spice yourself. For all ground spices, mix well and store in an airtight container.
2. Add spices to hot water for a Spiced tea, or lightly cook into ghee or your favourite cooking oil to drizzle on vegetables.
3. Sprinkle on foods while cooking or add to finished meals like soups, salads, sandwiches, stews, rice, casseroles, pasta dishes, vegetables, etc.

KAPHA MASALA SPICE MIX

AGGRAVATED KAPHA

Excess Kapha can become stubborn and lazy when thrown off balance. Kapha-type people gain weight and easily become obese.

Kapha are easily prone to allergies, colds, flu and asthma. They need to do regular exercise and watch their diet to stay fit.

According to Ayurveda, the **Kapha** dosha is a combination of the elements earth and water and governs the structure of the body, stabilising and protecting it. It has the quality of being heavy, slow, stuck and stubborn.

BENEFITS OF USING A KAPHA MASALA SPICE MIX

It will balance Kapha dosha and regulate weight gain by providing the energetic herbs to increase movement and vitality. It can improve slow digestion, which can make you lethargic, tired and stubborn and lead to toxins developing in the body that can create diabetes, high cholesterol, mucus and congestion, oedema, bloating and water retention.

It will help increase lightness of the body and the mind, lifting moods and heaviness, laziness, and stubbornness.

SIMPLE LIFESTYLE CHANGES

Kapha should have warm, light and dry food. Choose spicy, pungent, and bitter foods to enhance digestion, avoid heavy, oily foods, and reduce dairy and iced drinks.

Eat lighter foods, especially in the evening, and don't snack during the day—eat an apple. Warm spices help Kapha digestion and correct dosha imbalance. Drinking ginger tea helps, as well as reducing nuts and eating more seeds. Kaphas should not sleep during the daytime, and daily exercise, meditation and yoga are also important.

INGREDIENTS

- 3 tsp ground cumin *(Foundation Spice)*
- 2 tsp ground ginger
- 1 tsp black pepper
- 2 tsp turmeric
- 1 tsp ground coriander
- 2 tsp ground fennel

DIRECTIONS

1. Your spice mix will always taste better if you grind each spice yourself. For all spice mixes, mix well and store in an airtight container.
2. Add spices to hot water for a Spiced tea, or lightly cook into ghee or your favourite cooking oil to drizzle on vegetables. Sprinkle on foods while cooking or add to finished meals, soups, salads, sandwiches, stews, rice, casseroles, pasta dishes, vegetables, etc.

CHUTNEYS

Chutneys are considered a wonderful and important addition to Ayurveda meals. They offer a variety of positive aspects to food.

From the perspective of taste, they offer an exciting stimulation to the system, and providing nutritional benefits by using a variety of ingredients, from fresh fruits to nuts and dried fruits. They give us high doses of vitamins, especially C and A, and provide antioxidants in our daily eating.

According to Ayurveda principles of digestion, fresh fruit provides us with 'Ojas' (the vitality of life) and gives the body what it needs for digestion. It's recommended to bring all the six tastes into your daily meals, and chutneys enable this opportunity.

We can bring about balance in our food by the type of chutneys we eat and the fruit and spices that are included. This is a simple but very delicious chutney for all body types.

SIMPLE LEMON CHUTNEY PICKLE

This Simple Lemon Chutney Pickle is a tangy and flavourful addition that adds a burst of brightness to any dish. It's made with just a few ingredients, including lemons, salt, and spices like mustard seeds and chilli flakes. This chutney is quick and easy to prepare. It's versatile and adds a zest to a variety of dishes, and rice and dhal are great favourites.

INGREDIENTS

- 5-7 Lemons
- 2tbsp salt
- 1tbsp turmeric
- 1 tsp dosha masala
- ½ tsp chili

DIRECTIONS

1. Cut 5 lemons into small pieces keeping the juice – sprinkle and toss in the spice mix. Put into a clean jar and pour over all the juice, if you need more juice to cover then squeeze the remaining 2 lemons as required.
2. Shake well every day for 10 days or more. The longer the better.

PRUNE & GINGER CHUTNEY

The combination of prune and ginger offers a harmonious blend of flavours and health benefits, aligning well with Ayurvedic principles. Prunes, with their natural sweetness and rich fibre content, are known for their ability to support digestive health by promoting regularity and aiding in detoxification. Ginger is revered for its warming properties and potent medicinal qualities. This aromatic root is widely used in Ayurveda to kindle the digestive fire (Agni), stimulate circulation and alleviate digestive discomfort.

INGREDIENTS

- 8 prunes – soaked overnight or a tin of drained prunes
- ¾-inch fresh ginger 1 clove
- 6 cardamom seeds – NOT pods
- 1 pinch of black pepper

DIRECTIONS

Blitz all the ingredients together and decant them into a clean jar.

SIMPLE APPLE & DATE CHUTNEY

This is an ancient, traditional Ayurvedic chutney and using it as an addition to a meal makes it suitable for all doshas. Making a fresh chutney makes a simple dish wonderfully special. This all-purpose one can be done all year round using different herbs and spices for the season.

INGREDIENTS

- 1 large cooking apple, cored and chopped into small pieces
- ¼ cup of dates, chopped up
- ½ tsp ground cardamom
- ¼ tsp ground nutmeg
- 1 pinch of rock salt
- 1 tbsp grated ginger
- 1 tbsp ghee
- squeeze of lemon

DIRECTIONS

1. In a frying pan, sauté all the spices in the ghee for a minute until fragrant, then add the remaining ingredients and cook for 5 minutes or so until the desired consistency is to your liking.
2. Serve with salads, curries, vegetables and cheeses. Chutney is excellent for breaking up the fats in cheese.

NUT & CORIANDER CHUTNEY

This is a great recipe to make and perfect for the warmer weather. It's fine for all types, as we have made some alterations to the recipe.

Coriander, or cilantro as it's called in the USA, is a wonderful source of dietary fibre, manganese, iron and magnesium.

INGREDIENTS

- 1 cup of nuts, roasted and crushed in a mortar and pestle - Vata is OK with peanuts, Pitta with cashew nuts and Kapha with almonds
- 1 cup of chopped fresh coriander
- 2 cloves of crushed garlic – 1 for Pitta, 2 for Vata and Kapha types
- ½ tsp cumin seeds
- 1 tsp grated fresh ginger
- ½ tsp seeded crushed green chilli – none for Pitta
- 2 tbsp lemon juice
- 2 tbsp chopped fresh coconut *(optional but delicious)*
- salt and pepper, a pinch of each

DIRECTIONS

1. Roast the nuts with cumin seeds for a couple of minutes until fragrant, then crush in a mortar and pestle.
2. Separately crush the coriander, garlic, ginger and chilli (if using) in a mortar and pestle. Combine your seeds and nuts with your crushed spices, and add the lemon juice and seasoning (add optional coconut).
3. Serve on flatbread with feta cheese and pile the chutney on top or serve with a curry.

FLATBREADS

In Ayurveda, flatbreads are favoured for their lightness, digestibility and versatility. Unlike heavier, leavened breads, flatbreads are easier for the digestive system to process, making them ideal for promoting balanced digestion and avoiding digestive discomfort. Flatbreads serve as a convenient and nutritious addition for incorporating various herbs and spices for a holistic approach to nourishment and health maintenance. Flatbreads are valued in Ayurveda for their ability to provide sustenance and support digestive health.

Flatbreads are incredibly versatile and adaptable, making them a staple in Ayurveda cooking and offer endless possibilities. They can be filled, folded or topped with various ingredients, making them suitable for any meal or occasion. Easy to make and customise, flatbreads are good for their simplicity and ability to bring people together over delicious and satisfying meals.

QUINOA & HERB FLATBREAD

INGREDIENTS

- 1 cup cooked quinoa
- ¼ cup water
- ½ cup whole wheat flour (or any flour of your choice)
- 2 tablespoons ground flaxseeds
- ½ teaspoon salt
- herbs or spices for flavour (e.g., garlic powder, rosemary, thyme)

DIRECTIONS

1. Preheat your oven to 180/200°C.
2. In a blender or food processor, combine the cooked quinoa and water. Blend until smooth.
3. In a mixing bowl, combine the quinoa puree, flour, ground flaxseeds, salt, and any optional herbs or spices. Mix until a dough forms.
4. Place the dough on a floured surface and knead it for a few minutes until it becomes smooth.
5. Divide the dough into equal-sized portions and roll each portion into a ball.
6. Using a rolling pin, flatten each ball into a thin, round flatbread.
7. Place the flatbreads on a baking sheet lined with parchment paper.
8. Bake in the preheated oven for 15 minutes, or until the flatbreads are cooked through and slightly golden on the edges.
9. Remove from the oven and let them cool slightly before serving.

Enjoy your homemade quinoa flatbreads with the added nutritional boost of flaxseeds!

SIMPLE AYURVEDA VERSATILE CHAPATIS

Not many people can resist a warm rolled chapati filled with their favourite fillings. This traditional Indian dish is really easy and only takes a handful of ingredients.

Chapati is a type of Indian flatbread, and it's very popular in India. It is a staple and made of really simple ingredients: wheat flour, salt and water.

This is such a quick recipe and can be made for all kinds of meals. You simply add your favourite filling and enjoy good wholesome food. These little chapatis are made easily and quickly and eaten by families all over India.

It is packed with fibre and nutrition.

INGREDIENTS

- 2 cups of flour – *use good quality durum whole wheat flour if possible*
- ½ tsp salt
- 2 tbsp sesame oil

DIRECTIONS

1. Sift the flour with the salt and rub in the sesame oil. Add enough hot water to make a soft, pliable dough—usually, a small cupful.
2. Knead well and roll into a sausage shape so that you can cut off small pieces that you can roll into thin chapatis.
3. Cook both sides in a non-stick, dry pan until they are brown on both sides. After you have finished cooking, pile them on top of each other, ready to fill and serve.

FILLINGS

- fried potatoes
- mixed vegetables
- scrambled eggs/tofu
- fried bean sprouts and peanuts
- salads
- anything you fancy — enjoy!

DURUM WHOLE WHEAT FLOUR gives a wonderfully traditional taste to chapati and can be used to make other bread such as paratha, puri and roti.

We hope you found our Ayurveda Cookery Book enriching, nourishing and a source of wellness on your Ayurveda Journey.

Linda & Sandra

Find out more:
www.athomewithayurveda.com
www.ayurvedasage.com

Our social links:
@athomewithayurveda @homesweetholmedale
@athomewithayurveda @homesweetholmedale
@Linda Bretherton @Sandra Czachur

For courses, workshops and other information
email **info@athomewithayurveda.com**

[illegible]

[illegible]

[illegible]

[illegible]

Ingredients

- [illegible]
- [illegible] salt
- [illegible]

Directions

1. Stir the flour with the salt and mix in the [illegible] oil and enough hot water to make a soft, pliable dough—usually a small cupful.
2. Knead well and roll into a sausage shape so that you can cut off small pieces that you [illegible] into [illegible].
3. Cook both sides in a [illegible] until they are brown on both sides. After you have finished cooking, pile them on top of each other [illegible].

Fillings

- [illegible]
- mixed vegetables
- [illegible]
- [illegible] and [illegible]
- [illegible]

Printed in Great Britain
by Amazon

b36bb676-7c26-4014-9cce-64237466b664R01